The Bible On
The Church

The Bible

on

The Church

by D. DEDEN, S.C.J.

Translated by JOS. A. ROESSEN, S.C.J.

ST. NORBERT ABBEY PRESS
De Pere, Wisconsin
U. S. A.
1966

Nihil obstat:

Samuel D. Jadin, O. Praem.
Censor deputatus

Imprimatur:

†Stanislaus V. Bona, D.D.
Bishop of Green Bay
April 13, 1966

The *Nihil obstat* and *Imprimatur* are a declaration that a book or pamphlet is considered free from doctrinal or moral error. It is not implied that those who have granted the *Nihil obstat* and *Imprimatur* agree with the contents, opinions or statements expressed.

Originally published as
De Bijbel over de Kerk
Roermond and Maaseik, J. J. Romen & Zonen, 1962
Revised by author 1965

Library of Congress catalogue card number: 66 - 22815

Printed in the United States of America
ST. NORBERT ABBEY PRESS
De Pere, Wisconsin

CONTENTS

INTRODUCTION

The title of this book happily combines two subjects, which receive a great deal of attention today: the Bible and the Church. The constantly growing number of Bible clubs and church groups are proof of this. We see in this happy trend a reaction against the liberal and rationalistic tendencies of a past era, and against the materialism and mechanization of our own time; this was fostered by lay interest in theology and apostolate, post-war ecumenical openness and, above all, the impact of the recent Vatican Council II.

To establish a Biblical foundation for a doctrine on the Church naturally requires some exertion; this is increased if one wishes, in addition, to institute a comparison of the texts involved. The reader may find some consolation in the fact that our efforts to confine such a complex subject as the Church within the framework of a small book has certainly not been less exacting. It was necessary to limit the use of Bible texts to a minimum; many illuminating perspectives had to be overlooked; the net result is an outline rather than a treatise in depth. We shall trace in turn what the most important sections of the New Testament — the Gospels, Acts and the epistles of Paul — teach us about the Church. Although repetition is unavoidable, it is the only way to catch the different nuances; at times it is useful to show which elements should receive emphasis in the concept of the Church.

A concluding synthesis tries to be as truthful a reflection as possible of what the inspired writers of the New Testament teach about the Church.

The object of this book therefore is to establish a Biblical foundation for the mystery of the Church, and not to present a commentary on the **Constitution on the Church** of Vatican II. This Constitution nevertheless has a strong Biblical stance, especially in the first two chapters. To keep abreast, we shall have to keep this document constantly in mind; the Vatican Council, impelled by pastoral care, has emphasized certain factors seldom encountered in previous expositions about the Church. Thus the Church is in the eyes of the Council, no longer a static society, but rather a constantly-renewing living Church, standing in the center of history. This more dynamic view finds expression in the phrase "the People of God on the way," in the more active participation of the layman, in the freedom of religion, in ecumenical openness, in the changed attitude toward the Jews, etc. A study like this must consider the "aggiornamento" of the Church.

Hees-Nijmegen 1965

THE NAME "ECCLESIA"

Many of our contemporaries know the Church solely from the outside; for them it is a society of world-wide dimensions, kept together through one common belief and one common worship. Scripture however, which appeals to our faith, calls the Church a "mystery," once hidden in God, now revealed and partly come to realization (Eph. 1:9 ff.; Rom. 16:25 ff.). The Constitution on the Church therefore devotes its first chapter to this "Mystery." It is the mystery of a still sinful people which nevertheless possesses a guarantee of salvation because it is the extension of Christ's body: a mystery of a divine-human institution, in which man can find light, forgiveness and grace "to the praise of the glory of God" (Eph. 1:14).

To this institution early Christians gave the name "Church." Before we become fully absorbed in the organism, the Church, it may be profitable to consider the derivation of the word and its meaning. The most common names are germanic (Kirche — Church — Kerk — Kyrkan etc.) or from the romance language group (Eglise — iglesia — chiesa etc.). The first, to which our word "Church" belongs, reverts to the unbiblical Greek **kuriakon,** which means "house of the Lord"; the second from the Latin **ecclesia** reverts to the Biblical Greek **ekklesia.** Only this latter is of interest to us.

The word **ekklesia** occurs 125 times in the New Testament. Since the Church is the result only of God's salvific action through Christ, the term is rarely found in the Gospels (only twice in Matthew); it is used much more frequently by Paul (65 times), Acts (23 times), Revelation (20 times), John (3 times) and James (once). The current meaning can be best deduced especially from Paul.

What is the origin of the word? In profane Greek **ekklesia** meant a summoned people's assembly. In the Greek cities the herald summoned the people to assemble **(ek-kalein:** to summon, call up). It has no religious meaning; for their religious meetings the Greeks used other words. The origin of our term must therefore be sought elsewhere, namely in the Judaic tradition.

The Old Testament designated the Israelite community convened by Yahweh in the desert to adore him by two almost synonymous words: **qāhāl** and **ĕdāh.** The Septuagint invariably translates the first term **ekklesia,** the second **synagoga** — both followed by "of God." But in early Christendom "synagoga" had already taken on the meaning of a local Judaic community. Therefore the other term was the only one available for the first Christians. To differentiate from the synagogue they called themselves

ekklesia (the only exception: Jas. 2:2, "synagogue"). The stress on this word is always positive; it rests on the idea of the community of those who obey God's summons and not on the fact that those called are withdrawn from the world. It is the mission of the church to be in the world and to pass on God's call, and not to withdraw from it. By definition the Church is the opposite of a sect.

Ekklesia frequently occurs in Paul in the sense of local churches which gathered in a home; this, for instance, is indicated in the epistle headings. In Colossians and Ephesians however the universal church dominates. It is more or less accidental that in 1 Cor. the term is used in the Greek sense (on Grecian soil at that!) of "assembly"; in 1 Cor. 12-14 Paul is mainly concerned with reorganization of liturgical meetings. "Church" as "building" therefore does not come into the picture.

What is primary — the universal or the local church? This question is oversimplified and the reply is bound to be ambiguous. We see the facts in this way. One may agree that the Old Testament name **ekklesia** was first applied to the primeval community. This oldest core of Christianity was conscious that it was the messianic people of God of the final time (Acts 5:11; 8:1-3). As long as we remain in the Judaic-Christian world, there exists only one Church (cf. 9:31: "So the Church throughout all Judea and Galilee and Samaria had peace!"). Paul raged against this Church, i.e. the Judaic Christians. The situation changes only when a totally different

Christendom arises in Antioch, no longer of the
Judaic but of the gentile type; in imitation of the
primeval church it calls itself "the Church." Jerusalem however cannot see the Church as such in
this foundation: How could gentiles enter into the
"Church of God" without being circumcised? Con-
sequently "the Church" now becomes "church" and
one speaks of the "church that is in Jerusalem" and
the "church that is in Antioch" (Acts 11:22; 13:1).
The conversion of the gentiles constitutes the turning
point, and one begins to speak of (local) churches.
Paul identifies with this. It must still be proved
that he ever spoke of the universal church before his
letters which were written in prison. In the singular
or plural, he knows only local churches. With him
too the title of honor — "Church of God" — is reserved
for the Christians in Palestine (Gal. 1:13; 1 Cor. 15:9),
even in the plural form — "Churches of God" — (1
Thess. 2:14; 1 Cor. 11:16). The sole exception seems
to be that the Church of Corinth is also "Church
of God" (1 Cor. 11:22 included in the introduction,
1 Cor. 1:1 and its reiteration in 2 Cor. 1:1). But even
this appears to be, in view of this letter's repeated
allusions to the desert-time and the origins in Jerusalem, a conscious reference to the primeval community, which is held up as the ideal to the Corinthians. Paul very prudently takes into consideration,
in his preaching as well as in his collections, the position of Jerusalem and the communities in Palestine;
without the approval of, or at least permission from,
the superiors in Jerusalem he is fearful of going
astray. Only in his letters to the Colossians and

Ephesians — with the express assurance that the old barrier has gone — the last distinction between the Judaic church and the gentile church disappears and the "churches" retire from the field in favor of the one great universal Church. But it was a long, long way!

In summary we can say: in the Hellenistic world **ekklesia** was the summoned assembly; in the Old Testament it becomes the "assembly of God," the "community of God"; in the New Testament the title of honor "the community of God" is reserved for Christendom in Palestine; outside this are communities formed after the pattern of "this community of God"; finally, there is a consciousness that only the universal Church corresponds fully to the salvific plan of God.

2

THE CHURCH IN THE GOSPELS

The Kingdom of God

The word "church" does not occur in the gospels — with the exception Mt. 16:18 and 18:17. The synoptics use older terms such as "Kingdom of God" and "Kingdom of Heaven," which revert to the Old Testament.

Besides the supra-temporal and lasting dominion of Yahweh over the world, the Old Testament often mentions a future Kingdom of God that is to come in glory. Especially during and after the dark period of exile do the people eagerly await this salvific time. Ezekiel and Deutero-Isaias are the heralds of it, and the echo of their message can still be heard in Mal. 1:14; 1 Chron. 29:11; 2 Macc. 11:3-4; 22; 29; in Daniel and in a number of psalms, as Ps. 47; 93; 96-99.

Jesus recalls such Old Testament data, especially those in Daniel, when he teaches that the Kingdom of God is no earthly construct, but is self-revealing; when he makes a distinction between the already present Kingdom of God and the one of which the

full unfolding is still awaited; when he indicates that
the Kingdom of God is supposed to be a place (to
enter the Kingdom, to sit at the banquet, a place
opposite the gehenna, etc.), but in essence it means
the dominion of God — in other words, kingship
rather than kingdom.

On the one hand Jesus bears witness that the
Kingdom of God is still to come, and by this he
means God's definitive dominion, which begins at
the end of time, when with power he is to impose
his will on the people. The parables of the fishing net,
of the laborers in the vineyard, of the talents, etc.,
allude to this. The end of all these parables is to
show the division between the good and the bad, the
latter "to be thrown into the furnace of fire; there
men will weep and gnash their teeth" (Mt. 13:50). In
essence the Kingdom of God belongs to the hereafter. On the other hand, Jesus gives assurance that
with his coming the Kingdom of God has already
appeared. "The Kingdom of God is not coming with
signs to be observed; nor will they say, lo, here it is!
or there! for behold, the Kingdom of God is in the
midst of you" (Lk. 17:20 and 21). Jesus confirms
this assurance with deeds of power, healings, driving
out of devils, which form an integral element of his
message; this he especially underlines in his reply
to the disciples of John (Mt. 11:4 ff.).

The Kingdom of God appears to be a mystery, and
because it announces itself not only through but also
in the God-made-Man, his person shares in this
mystery. The question is: what is Jesus' place during

the time between the beginning and final completion of the Kingdom of God? His announcement
that "the Kingdom of God is at hand," does not end
with a triumphal march and a stately accession to the
throne but on a cross, on which he, the King of
Israel, gives his life. The whole drama of his action
before the people is enacted round this "rock of
stumbling" upon which the disciples themselves trip:
"The Son of Man will be delivered into the hands of
men, and they will kill him, and after three days he
will rise" (Mk. 8:31; 9:31). This is stated even more
strongly! Precisely because Jesus calls himself Messiah,
Son of God, and claims to be King of the Kingdom of
Heaven, he is cast out and crucified as "King of the
Jews." Thus the mystery of the Kingdom of God
is not just hidden in the person of him who announces and brings it; there is mystery also in this
that it commences after his departure. He arose after
his redeeming death on the cross, and ascended to
the right hand of the Father, where he rules the
universe as omnipotent King (Lk. 24:26; Mt. 28:18).
The dominion of Christ dates therefore from his
ascension, so that the Holy Spirit can testify at Pentecost through the mouths of the apostles: "God has
made him both Lord and Christ, this Jesus whom
you crucified" (Acts 2:36).

What is called the "Kingdom of God" is therefore
not exactly the same as what we understand by
"Church"; its extension is greater. The Church is
only the earthly stage of the Kingdom of God; it
is its organ, or, more precisely, its sacrament. The

object of the Church is to make the Kingdom of God sacramentally present, as a salvific sign adapted to the time between Christ's resurrection and parousia. This means two things: that the embodiment of the Kingdom of God in the Church is transitory and shall one day make way for the full revelation of God's dominion in eternity; secondly, that the Kingdom of God is also to be found outside the Church. The Church truly is the certain sign of the presence of the Kingdom of God; outside it this presence remains in some degree anonymous, problematic and uncertain, either because of the effects of sin, or because of the specific character of its different spheres of operation. True, sin is also found in the Church, but it cannot remove the presence of the Kingdom; on the contrary, in the Church sin encounters the opposition by which it is overcome.

The Church is therefore the revelation of the Kingdom — but in secrecy. Seen in a purely human way, the Church may seem weak and insignificant; the fact is that this Church, in which sinners are found, withstands the powers of hell, is a "sign" of the power that is and works within her; her unity and sanctity are indeed a sign of God in history.

The Kingdom of God, seen in this light, is not the same as what we call "Church." The Church makes the Kingdom in fact present in history in what might be called its earthly beginning. But when Christ speaks of the Kingdom of God as one which really begins only on the day of judgment, is it possible to claim that Christ instituted a Church? Yes indeed that is possible! Jesus regarded himself as the Messiah; there is no Messiah without a messianic community. He showed himself as shepherd; there can be no shepherd without a flock. He called himself the Son of Man; the Son of Man in Daniel 7, to which he alludes, is not only the heavenly king of the future, but also the representative of the messianic people, the saints of the Most High, who share in his privileges. Of course Jesus did not institute his Church at one particular moment; all his activities were directed toward this. One can however discern in his actions some decisive phases. Of these, three are most important: the selection of the twelve, the promise to Peter at Caesarea Philippi and the Last Supper. The decisive moments in which the Church goes from promise to reality are Easter and Pentecost; but one must see these in the perspective of Jesus' earthly action.

According to the synoptics, all Jesus' endeavors were directed to the formation of a lasting religious community which would remain after his death and continue his mission. This community is constituted by belief in Jesus, confession of this belief, and a following of Christ prepared to suffer even death (Mk. 8:34-38 par.; Mt. 10:26-39). Here we have an essential difference from the action of earlier divine messengers, such as the Old Testament prophets and John the Baptist; these demanded only belief in God, but did not make their own person the center of their mission. Jesus demands of his followers an attitude of mind toward himself which essentially forms the foundation of a lasting worship and the durable belief of a religious community (cf. the institution narratives of the new covenant, especially Lk. 22:15, 18, 20). The supreme authority with which Jesus preaches his doctrine points in the same direction; this departs from the traditional in important ways, and is on a level with divine revelation itself (Sermon on the Mount; Mt. 7:29, etc.). Jesus was fully aware that such action was bound to bring about a division, not only among his followers and Judaism in Palestine (Mk. 2:21 ff.; Mt. 8:10-12; 21:43) but also in the strongest sectors of society (Mt. 10:34-39). The constitution of this community is love of one's neighbor. Symbol and expression of this unity and belief are the rites of baptism (Mt. 28:17) and the Eucharist (institution narratives).

Spiritual, visible, lasting and universal

The synoptic gospels draw for us a complete picture of how Christ founded a **spiritual** kingdom with a **visible** structure and a **lasting** destiny. These three points deserve to be considered more in detail.

Characteristic of the **spiritual nature** of the new Kingdom of God is the total banishment of all earthly and political pretensions, of all that the old Judaic theocracy clung to so firmly. Therefore, no political Messiah! Jesus himself refuses to use the title in public; he forbids others to propagate the idea of Messiah, thus precluding an ever-threatening explosive nationalism. This ban quiets the enthusiasm engendered by his miracles and preaching. Finally the tide ebbed; as Messiah, Jesus fails. Then he begins to concern himself with his apostles. They at least have accepted him as Messiah. He explains to them the sense in which he is the Messiah: not one equipped with worldly power, who will free his people by force of arms from the Roman occupation, but a humble and meek Messiah come to give his life for them. He predicts his passion, death and resurrection for them.

As spiritual leader Jesus does not just command and prohibit, as the rabbis did. The Sermon on the Mount with its beatitudes and its heroic virtues (especially love for one's neighbor) is primarily a doctrine of perfection. The groundwork of the New Covenant is the introvertedness of the Old Law, which had become fixed in the juridical and the external. The letter remains but the application is new, thanks to the creative spirit of the new Moses. In solemn cadence a repeatedly recurring theme sounds in our ears: "You have heard that it was said (namely by Moses) . . . but I say to you . . .!" (Mt. 5:27-48).

The demand required to enter the Kingdom of God is equally spiritual: "to become like a child" (Mt. 18:3 ff.). To become like a child means to be open with God, and not to cling to what one is, or seems to be, or possesses. For precisely that reason the Kingdom of God belongs to the poor (Mt. 5:3); they know that they possess nothing to call their own. Therefore publicans and prostitutes will enter before obvious bigots (Mt. 21:31) because they are conscious that they are nothing before God. Therefore

the children of the Kingdom (the chosen people) are
cast out (Mt. 8:12; Lk. 13:28) while many from east
and west and north and south enter, because the
children of the Kingdom are perpetrators of iniquities
toward God.

The great adversary is satan. Jesus must take his
kingdom from him. Not content with his victory
over satan, when he tempts him in vain to become a
worldly Messiah (Mt. 4:1-11 par.), he wants to
snatch his prey from him. He declares that he has
come to seek what is lost (Mt. 19:10). He cures
the possessed; Mark seems to show the devils flee in
fright at every step of Jesus. Jesus himself suggests
his victory over satan as a proof that the Kingdom
of God has come on earth (Mt. 12:28); he arms his
disciples against the devils (Lk. 19:17-20).

But the spiritual nature of the Kingdom of God
does not require that it be invisible. It was never
alleged that the Church consists solely of saints and
predestined, with no one knowing who they are.
This would be absolutely incorrect. That she lives
in hearts and souls is of course true, but that she
forms a **visible** society, clearly distinguished from
every other group, is also true. This the Old Testament establishes; it portrays the people of the final
time as a city on a mountain (Is. 2:2-4; Mich. 4:1-5),
as a fully lighted city (Is. 49:6-10), as a high tree to
which all birds come to make their nests (Ezek.
17:22-24). Other prophetic figures, — a people,
kingdom, vineyard, flock, temple — point in the
same direction. Jesus uses a metaphor for visibility

when he compares his disciples with a fully visible city on a mountain, and with the light of the world (Mt. 5:14-16). They are known as disciples, and for just that reason they are persecuted (Mt. 10:17-22 and par.). The compulsory character of baptism clearly indicates that the Church, into which one can enter only through this externally visible rite, is itself a visible society. The hierarchy will later establish the evidence for this.

Duration and **universality** belong together. If the Kingdom of God is not lasting, then it could not be meant for all people; if it is for all people, then its means of grace must be adapted to all times.

Jesus repeatedly directs the attention of his hearers to the future life. The Kingdom of God will reach completion only when all will have submitted; only then will the faithful have priceless gifts showered upon them. End of the world and parousia, resurrection and judgment, eternal life and damnation — these are the "last things" which the Christian must constantly keep in mind in order to conform his conduct to them. It is the final phase of Kingdom of God, and it is essentially eschatological. The question however is: Does the Kingdom of God coincide completely with the hereafter? The affirmative was defended by the old eschatological school. The gospel however teaches differently; it recognizes that the actual, ideal final phase is preceded by the present, earthly phase, which is of indefinite duration and will one day pass into the heavenly phase.

Does not Jesus declare, with reference to his

miracles and casting out of devils, that the Kingdom of God is already here (Mt. 11:1-12; 12:28) and that this silently growing kingdom (Lk. 17:20 ff.) is something entirely different from the glorious return of the Son of Man at the end of the world (17:23-27)?

The day of this return is known only to the Father (Mt. 24:26); even the Son, who knows everything he reveals from the Father, has received no mandate to make it known (Mk. 13:32; Acts 1:7). That day will come like a thief in the night, overtake mankind as the flood overtook the contemporaries of Noah. Therefore one needs to watch, be constantly on guard . . .

Thus it is impossible to date the return and to establish duration of the Church. But that this may be a long time is obvious from the parables of the mustard seed, which grows into a large tree, in which birds can build their nests (Mk. 4:32), the slowly working leaven (Mt. 13:33), and the field where grain and weeds grow together till harvest time (Mt. 13:24 ff.). Several texts state that the Church will exist as long as the world. She is the building on the rock, against which "the gates of hell shall not prevail" (Mt. 16:18). Elsewhere the Master says: "I will pray the Father, and he will give another Counsellor, to be with you for ever" (Jn. 14:16); for ever, i.e. as long as the world exists. The gospel of St. Matthew ends: "Go therefore and make disciples of all nations . . . and lo, I am with you always, to the close of the age" (28:19 ff.). On the one hand the apostles must teach all nations; on the other hand "always" supposes at least that this will take a long time. The Church will therefore remain as long as there are people on earth; this is necessary because God wants to save everyone.

Did Jesus intend to teach the gentiles as well? The Gospel states two facts: Jesus limits his own preaching to Israel, but he gives his apostles the whole world as a field of action. This universality was predicted. In Abraham all nations would be blessed (Gen. 12:1-3; 18:18; 22:15 ff.). Later prophecies elaborated this promise in different ways, especially in the form of a world-wide Kingdom with Jerusalem as capital. They presented the conversion of the gentiles as the fruit of the sufferings of the servant of Yahweh (Is. 42:1-6; 49:6; 52:15; 53:11 ff.; Ps. 22:27-32). One could not therefore expect that Christ, in whom all these prophecies were to be fulfilled, would be indifferent to the fate of the gentiles.

This supposition is ultimately confirmed by the supranational position of this doctrine; it has no enmity toward foreign powers: one must give to Caesar what is Caesar's. Jesus' doctrine is so universally human; he addresses himself to things of the soul and banishes all nationalism. This is no national Messiah, there is no national stance in his protrayal of the Kingdom of God: to obey God is all that is required. To bring about love for God, no appeal is made to the deliverance from Egypt, nor to God's miracles in the desert. No; God is Father because he is creator and redeemer; he asks childlike love from all men. As his children we are bound to love each other as brothers and sisters. The parables also speak of a universal Kingdom. The field which is sown is the world; the mustard seed which grows up to a large tree offers room for all birds. The disciples are to be the salt of the earth, the light of the world.

Personally, Jesus takes no part in the mission to the gentiles. His territory is Israel. When he now and then crosses the border, it is to go into hiding and to rest. In Syro-Phoenicia he does not preach and he performs no miracles (Mk. 7:24-30 par.); his reply to the Canaanite woman sounds like a refusal (Mt. 15:24 ff.).

Nevertheless the gentiles are not excluded. The Canaanite and the royal official are used as examples because of their faith. Precisely because of this faith, Jesus insists: "Many will come from east and west and sit at table with Abraham and Isaac and Jacob in the Kingdom of Heaven; while the sons of the Kingdom will be thrown into the outer darkness" (Mt. 8:11 ff.; cf. Lk. 13:28 ff.). His prediction of the rejection of the Jews and the calling of the gentiles is seen again in the parable of the unworthy laborer in the vineyard (Mt. 21:43 par.), of the wedding feast (Mt. 22:7-10 par.) and in the discourse on the end of Jerusalem (Mt. 24:14 par.). In John we find the same universality. The Lamb of God comes to take away the sin of the world (1:29). God has so loved the world that he gave his only begotten Son, that whoever believes in him will not perish but have eternal life (3:16-19); etc.

So the conversion of the gentiles formed part of the messianic program; Jesus charged his apostles to carry this out (Mt. 28:18-20). He did this not as counsel, nor as a wish, but as a command binding them and their successors "until the end of time" to proclaim the good tidings throughout the whole world. They are not to wait till the nations come to them, but have to set out ("go"). They are not to give just superficial talks; they must transform cate-chumens into true disciples of Christ (**matheusate** =make into disciples). This command to convert has occasionally been called an invention of early Christendom, trying to justify what had been in use. But what is new is only the form. What Christ had long before introduced as prophecy he now formu-lates in an explicit command. Was that not entirely in the line of development? Backing up the testimony of Matthew we find Mark (16:15; if this text is not his own, it is at least very old) and Luke (Acts 1:8).

Apostolic rule

After a night spent in prayer, Jesus chooses his **apostles** from his group of disciples, by calling each one by name (Mt. 10:1-4 par.). In conformity with the tribes of Israel he chooses twelve; they will be the twelve chieftains of the spiritual Israel. Jesus himself calls them "apostles" or ambassadors. Mark characterizes their role in two concepts: Jesus chooses them to be with him and he sends them out; in other words, they are to be his companions and later his witnesses (Mk. 3:14). Their mission in Galilee, directly after their election, is the prelude to their final mission by which Jesus shall live on in them. Jesus concentrates on these twelve. He explains the parables to them (Mk. 4:10); he takes them aside to initiate them into the mystery of his passion and death (Mt. 20:17). He teaches these future ministers how to serve in humility and love (Mt. 18:1-4; 20:20-28 par.). They alone are allowed at the Last Supper, participate in the Eucharist, and receive the power to renew this mystery. He reveals himself to them in the intimacy of the cenacle. Though his capture totally upsets them, his resurrection encourages them again; this becomes the unshakable foundation on which the faith of the Church will rest. After they are instructed about the Kingdom of God by the risen Savior for a last time, they form the nucleus of the primitive community. All this makes it obvious that Jesus meant them to be his successors, as leaders of the community he founded.

In Mt. 18, an instruction on the Church, a passage appears about fraternal correction (18:15-18). Serious effects seem to indicate a serious offense. With all possible prudence one tries to undo it. He begins with a private warning. If this does not help, he then brings in — to make an impression — some witnesses. If this has no effect, then the Church is drawn in. Should even this fail, then he is to be considered a heathen and publican. This cannot be misunderstood: to treat a brother as the Jews treated heathens and publicans, means to avoid every religious and, where possible, every social association with them. How is the Church to make this decision? By appointing a jury? The following verse gives the answer: "Amen I say to you, if you forgive the sins of any, they are forgiven; if you retain the sins of any, they are retained."

These words, first addressed to Peter alone (Mt. 16:19), are now directed to all the apostles. With this Jesus does not retract what he had granted to Simon; he extends these rights to his colleagues, leaving the primacy aside. In connection with the above-mentioned sin, "bind and loose" is the same as retain and forgive, inflict punishment or remit. Apart from this it means much more; it includes not only the judicial power, but the magisterial and legislative power as well. All decisions on earth will be ratified in heaven: in other words, God forgives or condemns through the apostles, teaches through them, binds through them. This privilege is given to them in the interest of the Church; it is a means to protect and guide her. She must therefore profit by it, even when the twelve have gone.

If we may also bring in the fourth gospel for a moment we see it develop in its own way. We hear nothing about Church or Kingdom of God, but hear only about "the life" which is much more spiritual and more universal. Although the Church is not mentioned as such, her attributes are underlined in the high-priestly prayer (Jn. 17). Jesus wishes her to be **"one"**: in her and through her all the faithful form one union with him; outside her no one can come to him or to the Father. He wishes her to be **"holy"**: he sacrifices himself to sanctify his apostles in their mission. He wishes her to be **"catholic"**: he sends her over all the earth. Finally, he wishes her to be **"apostolic"**: he prays only "for those who believe through their word" (17:20), thereby making it known that there can be no other true belief than that which comes from the apostles.

The day before his death Jesus offered himself in order to gain necessary graces for his apostles, so that they might be able to continue his mission. After his resurrection he entrusts them with the fruits of his sacrifice by appointing them: "Peace be with you. As the Father has sent me, even so I send you" (20:21). With this they become plenipotentiaries of Christ and his Father. "And when he had said this, he breathed on them and said to them, Receive the Holy Spirit. If you forgive the sins of any, they are forgiven; if you retain the sins of any, they are retained." The breath symbolizes the reality and spiritual nature of the power he imparts to them; this is especially attributed to the Holy Spirit. It consists in the forgiveness of sins. The Master leaves it to his servants to determine the conditions for it. This authorization can be exercised in different ways, for example, through baptism; but direct forgiveness with power and judgment, dealt with here, takes place in the sacrament of penance and is dependent upon the priestly power.

In the passage mentioned Jesus imparts the Spirit to his apostles in regard to forgiveness of sins. In the cenacle he had promised them the same Spirit who descended upon them on Pentecost to help them in a dual function: the task of teacher (Jn. 14:16 ff., 25 ff.; 16:12-15) and of witness (15:26 ff.; 16:5-11). Since they are witnesses the Spirit will assist them to testify to Christ, and he will make his presence in the faithful known through perceptible signs. Since they are teachers, he will "teach everything" to them, and will bring back to their minds all that Jesus told them (4:26) and "lead them to the truth" (16:13) and gradually direct them into the full content of Jesus' teaching.

This teaching mandate had already been given the apostles in the mission-command of Mt. 28:18-20, quoted above.

From the preceding it is clear that the Church, according to the gospels, is not a democratic but a hierarchic institution; it consists of subjects and rulers. There is still the question whether there are degrees of authority in the governing body. Do the apostles possess their power independently of each other with no other mutual connection than the Holy Spirit? Or is there a leader among them, so that the hierarchy is at the same time a monarchy?

Primacy

Three gospel texts give the answer to this by referring to the primacy of Peter. Mt. 16:17-19 shows that the Savior promised Peter a primacy which was more than one of honor; it also guarantees a position of power over the whole Church: Lk. 21:30 ff. and Jn. 21:15 ff. state that this promised leadership was really conferred upon Peter. It is striking that all the evangelists acknowledge the precedence of Peter; the only one who does not mention this transfer of power is he who is considered to be the echo of Peter's preaching.

For the primacy of Peter the so-called Petrine-text of Mt. 16:17-19 must be considered first. "Simon Peter replied, You are the Christ, the Son of the living God. And Jesus answered him, Blessed are you Simon Bar-Jona! For flesh and blood has not revealed this to you, but my Father, who is in heaven. And I tell you, you are Peter, and on this rock I will build my church, and the powers of death shall not prevail against it. I will give you the keys of the Kingdom of Heaven and whatever you bind on earth shall be bound in heaven, and whatever you loose on earth shall be loosed in heaven."

That the text really belongs in the gospel of Matthew is clear from the fact that it figures in all the Greek manuscripts and in all the old translations. Confirmation is found in this that it unmistakably bears Matthew's stamp. We offer some data as illustration. Although the beatitudes are not mentioned by Matthew alone, he shows his preference for them; in the Sermon on the Mount he uses nine verses (5:3-11) as compared to four in Luke (6:20-22). "Bind and loose" combined with "on earth and in heaven" is used in Matthew 18:18; it is not found elsewhere in the New Testament. "The Father who is in heaven" and "the heavenly Father" appear in Matthew twenty-three times, in Mark and Luke only once; even in the "Our Father" Luke omits this title. Finally, only Matthew speaks about "Kingdom of Heaven"; Mark and Luke use "Kingdom of God."

Another question is whether these words in Matthew are indeed spoken by Jesus himself. The text certainly goes back to the primeval community. That they must be Jesus' own words is therefore obvious. The promise to make his disciples fishers-of-men, the choice of the twelve from a much larger number, their appointment as apostles and the mission-command, the reference to the still small flock (Luke 12:32), the charge to Peter to confirm his brethren after his own conversion (Luke 22:32) — all indicate that the building of the Church upon Peter is no foreign element in Jesus' doctrine. Add to this, that Jesus, at the first meeting, gave to Simon — not only according to Matthew but also according to the other gospels — the prophetic name Cephas or Rock. This had nothing to do with his character (as for instance the name "Sons of Thunder"); it could therefore be meaningful only in regard to his function. This first meeting is beautifully depicted by John: "He first found his brother Simon, and said to him, We have found the Messiah (which means Christ). He brought him to Jesus. Jesus looked at him and said, So you are Simon the son of John; you shall be called Cephas (which means Peter)" (Jn. 1:41 and 42). The points of comparison between this text and the "Petrine-text" are immediately apparent. Both speak of "Messiah" or the Christ, of "Simon Bar-Jona" and of the new name "Peter." Moreover, both put a connection between Simon's new name

and Jesus' title: John does so by first giving the
Aramaic original and then the Greek translation of
both names; Matthew does this in dialogue form:
Who do you say I am . . . I tell you who you are.
Thus the historicity of the Petrine-text is indirectly
confirmed by John.

If one believes that this logion without doubt
bears the stamp of Matthew and thus must go back
to Jesus himself, has not the evangelist given it the
wrong place in Jesus' life? Does it not stand there
in flagrant contradiction with verses 22-23 immediately following? First there is highest praise: "Blessed
are you Simon"; immediately after this comes a
vehement scolding. "Get behind me satan." Do not
these two texts exclude one another? Especially
since the second appears in Mark but, the first does
not?

Matthew is known for joining disparate elements,
as for instance he does in the Sermon on the Mount.
This logion too certainly has an isolated character,
but this isolation is literary in nature rather than
essential, as has just been shown. The difficulty
thus exists only in the silence of Mark and Luke.
Like Matthew, they also relate the confession of
Peter in Caesarea (Mk. 8:29; Lk. 9:20). Jesus' only
reply is to charge his apostles to keep silent about
this title; this is followed by a more precise exposition of his messianic function which will culminate
in his passion and death; he then counsels the
multitude to follow him despite the sacrifices this
entails. How is the silence about this very important

promise of the primacy to be explained? This at-
tracted attention in antiquity. The silence of Mark,
spiritual son and mouthpiece of Peter, created utmost
surprise. But precisely this intimate relationship
provided an explanation: the reserve of Mark is
occasioned by the modesty of his master. Eusebius
of Caesarea, who makes himself the sounding-board
of tradition says: "Peter eagerly related what humil-
iated him, as for example the "Get behind me, satan"
and his threefold denial; but he was carefully silent
about everything that exalted him. Mark, who re-
produces Peter's preaching, adhered to this and left
the sweet odor of humility to him." As for Luke,
he reserved for himself the right to communicate
a hitherto unedited document about Peter's primacy
(see further on) and thus could consider himself free
to deal here with the same theme. This procedure
Luke used more often.

Let us restrict ourselves for a few moments to
the meaning of our text. Like Mary before him
(Luke 1:45), Peter now is called blessed for his
faith. Jesus' person and salvific function can be
known only through revelation (Mt. 11:25 ff.). Peter
owes his new insight not to flesh and blood, not to
weak and fallible men, but to God. Blessed is he,
who is chosen by God for such a thing, and accepts
it with a believing heart.

After his confession as to who Jesus really is, the
Master unfolds the grandiose plans which Providence
has in store for him. "And I tell you, you are Peter."
The apostles usually called Simon by this previously

unknown name which means "Rock." It is a symbolic
name which points to the function awaiting him:
to be the foundation of a building.

"And on this rock I will build my Church." The
idea of building upon a rock is not strange (Mt.
7:24-27 par.); neither is it unusual that someone
should be symbolized as a rock. Abraham is once
called this (Is. 51:1 ff.); elsewhere it always designates God: he who is the strength itself and makes
others strong. For an unbiased reader it is obvious,
and today seldom disputed, that "rock" here alludes
to Simon himself and not to his inflexible character,
nor to his strength, nor to his faith to which he
has just given proof. Simon will, as rock, make the
Church unshakable and one, or — without metaphor
— become her leader vested with power. The Greek
word for "Church," as we have seen, is the ordinary
Septuagint translation of the Hebrew qāhāl, which
in the Old Testament stands for the community of
Yahweh. According to Is. 28:14-16 God gave his Son
to this community as foundation — a statement with
which early Christendom readily agreed (Rom. 9:33;
10:11; 1 Pet. 2:6). Jesus could rightly here call
the people of God of the final time "his" Church.
The privilege of Peter does not alter that fact. The
sovereignty of Christ would be lessened if he were
denied the right and power to choose a deputy.
Although he himself incontestably remains the sole
foundation (1 Cor. 3:1), he delegates his power to
his visible deputy on earth. By saying that he "will
build" the people of God, Jesus imitates the meta-

phor of the Old Testament which calls the people of Israel the "house of Jacob" and even the "house of God"; this term also alludes to a new building which will not only remain but will replace the old Israel. This old Israel is rejected (21:43-46) and the new may no longer be restricted to one nation. The Church is not a Jewish sect.

Let us consider "Gates of Hell." Gates are a symbol of the strength of a city. For "Hell" the Greek uses "Hades," underworld. This can be conceived as the kingdom of death; thus the Church of Christ receives the promise of imperishability. Hell can also be taken as the kingdom of the devil. This is more in harmony with the militant role (gates, overcome) awarded to Hades. It sees the Church as standing against it on the foundation of Peter. Then it is house against house, satan's kingdom against the Kingdom of Christ, to which the whole gospel gives witness. This struggle awaits the Church not only in the form of opposition and persecution, but also from within through scandal, heresy and schism; but she will never succumb.

The power of the keys is a figure of supreme authority, (cf. Is. 22:22). The bearer of the keys can admit or exclude. It is Peter's right to open or close the entrance to the Kingdom of Heaven in its earthly phase of the Church as well as in its heavenly stage. The words "bind and loose" are technical terms used by the rabbis, which refer to means of correction by which someone was condemned (bound) or acquitted (loosed). Taken in this sense of refusing (bind) or permitting (loose), Peter will be entrusted with absolute doctrinal power and absolute legal and administrative power over the new people of God, and his decision will be valid before God.

Of course, the function of Peter as head does not exclude the rights of the other apostles. Matthew 18:18 awards the power of binding and loosing to the twelve; when Peter receives the privilege of the personal title of "Rock" and "Key-Bearer," this means that he is also the leader of the twelve in this respect.

That Matthew 16:18-19 does not explicitly speak about succession need not be a surprise. Texts of prophetic caliber like these leave chronological stages rather hazy. Something similar takes place in the final text of Matthew: "Go and make disciples of all nations . . ." (Mt. 28:19), where Christ gives assurance that he will remain with his apostles to the end of the world. Nevertheless, no one will deny that this divine assistance also extends to their successors. It is true that it explicitly says "to the end of the world." Does the promise "the gates of hell shall not prevail against her" mean something different?

Although the Petrine-text speaks of a **personal** privilege, inasmuch as this is awarded only to Peter, by-passing the other apostles, it is nevertheless not concerned with the personal elevation of Peter, but with the **existence and continuity of the messianic salvific community.** It concerns the primary function which is necessary and lasting. This constitutional element of the Church affects not only her institution but her essential structure. Function, for the Church, is just as necessary as foundation for a building. Peter must continue his indispensable role in his successors after his departure from earthly life.

This is confirmed by views of the Judaic-Palestinian milieu where Jesus uttered his words. Here one could not think of the continuance of the Israelite community without succession of leadership. Moses appointed Joshua as his successor; the pontificate of Aaron was hereditary, and since the time of David the same applied to kingship. In the thinking of Christians converted from Jewry, leadership over the new people of God must have raised the thought of succession.

A second primary text is Luke 22:31 ff. "Simon, Simon, behold satan demanded to have you, that he might sift you like wheat, but I have prayed for you that your faith may not fail; and when you have turned again, strengthen your brethren."

These words are spoken in the cenacle. Jesus puts his prayer against the demands of satan. He does not ask that his followers be spared from temptation, because God wants to save the world through suffering; he asks for strength. This is remarkable! While all the apostles are threatened, Jesus prays only for Peter. He must become the buoy for all. Jesus prayed that his faith might not fail. From this we may conclude at what the devil was aiming: that the

gruesome humiliations of Jesus' passion and death
would undermine their faith. The fundamental value
of this faith is evident from this satanic design and
from Jesus' prayer. Because Peter is to be the
foundation of the Church, Jesus prayed for his
faith. Peter's coming fall, to which Jesus alludes,
will be more a lack of courage than a wavering of
his faith. As though Jesus forgives him in advance,
he appoints him mediator for his brethren.

Like the Petrine-text this passage also speaks of
conflict between Church and hell, of the same care
of Jesus for his followers, and of the same role of
Peter. In our text this is faith and authority. Peter
will be for his brethren what Jesus was for him.
Through Peter Jesus will impart certainty and
strength to the others: it is of this that Matthew
speaks.

The primacy promised to Peter after his confession in Caesarea and later on the eve of Jesus' passion is finally assigned to him with solemnity after
the resurrection. The text asserting this is John
21:15-19.

The authenticity of John 21 is contested; probably
this chapter is the work of a disciple-editor. The
matter has not yet been decided. But — directly
or indirectly — the story goes back to an eye-witness
(21:24); the elders of the Church in Asia vouch for
his trustworthiness (21:24b).

The miraculous catch of fish (vv. 1-14), which
introduces the appointment of Peter, is not without

hints of the primacy in this symbolizing gospel. The
other apostles immediately accept the invitation to
go fishing; the action takes place in Peter's boat;
it is he who is told that the stranger on the shore
is no one else than the Lord; it is he who first
hastens to him, thus showing his great love.

Then follows his appointment as chief shepherd
(vv. 15-17). The threefold questioning reminds him
of his threefold fall. Jesus does not ask him to
renew the confession of faith he gave in Caesarea; his
fall was not the result of a lack of faith but of
courage. Nor was there question of forgiveness —
this had already been given him. Jesus asks about
his love, because Christian authority is a serving,
a giving of self. The Master himself went to the
extreme; he expects greater love from his first deputy
than from the others.

Less arrogant now than he was before his fall,
Peter prefers not to compare himself with others;
instead he appeals three times to Jesus' own convic-
tion: "You know that I love you." Jesus' persistence
grieves him; the third time he asserts: "Lord, you
know everything; you know that I love you." Beautiful simplicity of manly love! Three times he will
hear Jesus depute pastorship, care and defense of
the flock as a whole to him. From now on no one
will be able to maintain that he follows Jesus if he
does not obey Peter.

In the final verses (21:18-23) the primacy of Peter
receives a particular luster through the halo of his

martyr death. There is no stronger proof of his
dedication than the sacrifice of his life. Where the
Master leads the way, there his disciple will follow.

This Church, instituted in the world and extended
as a visible entity governed by the successor of Peter
and the bishops united with him, is recognizable
in the Catholic Church. But many elements of
sanctification and truth are also found outside her;
these, as proper gifts of Christ's Church, lead to
Catholic unity. According to the Constitution on
the Church (No. 8) she has to fill a particular role
in the present world.

After his departure Jesus will continue his witness
on earth, and this he accomplishes through his
Church. For this witness to be authentic it must
bear his seal. Just as he executed the work of redemption in poverty (Lk. 9:58), self-denial (Mt.
8:18-22) and persecution (Jn. 15:18-27), so the Church
is called to tread the same road of humility (Mt. 18:3),
the washing of feet (Jn. 13:13 ff.), in order to pass
on the fruits of salvation to man. The Good Shepherd
has not come to be served, but to serve (Mt. 20:28;
Mk. 10:45) and to give his life for his sheep (Jn.
10:11). The same is expected from the leaders of the
Church. Far from reaching for earthly glory, the
task of the Church consists in total servitude
(diakonia). Jesus enjoined this upon his apostles;
rulers of nations wish to be regarded as benefactors
and masters, but if they follow his example they
will have to be servants of all (diakonos; Mk. 10:42
ff. par.).

Christ was sent by the Father "to preach the good news to the poor . . . and to proclaim release to the captives" (Lk. 4:18), ". . . to seek and save the lost" (Lk. 19:10). Hence the Church must surround with love all who have met with human weakness. Much more is demanded! As the Church of the poor she must recognize in the poor and suffering the image of her poor and suffering Founder (Mt. 25:35-40). Christ was the Holy One of God and without guilt (Jn. 6:69; 8:46); he came only to expiate the misdeeds of his people. The Church who bears sinners within her bosom must strive incessantly after repentance and renewal of life in order to remain the salt of the earth and the light of the world (Mt. 5:13-16).

3

THE CHURCH IN THE
ACTS OF THE APOSTLES

The people of God

Some have held that Jesus was a Jewish Messiah and reformer, but never had the intention of instituting a Church. They hold that this is the work of Paul: result, an impassable chasm between the historical Jesus and the Catholic Church! The Acts of the Apostles, which describe the origin and growth of the Church are an indispensable link between the gospels and the letters of Paul.

The Acts show the Church of Jerusalem as one great religious family. This is continuity with the old Israel; the salvific promises of the Old Testament are fulfilled in Christ (2:31 etc.) and in the gift of God, the Holy Spirit (2:16 ff.). But there is a breach with unbelieving Judaism, or, more clearly, with the Jews who cease to be the people of God as long as they reject the consequences of the faith of their fathers. The Church differs from Judaism in her confession that "Jesus is the Lord and Messiah" whom the Jews have crucified (2:36), but whom God has raised from the dead (2:24 etc.). For this reason the Christians of Jerusalem do not consider themselves a Jewish sect, but the true Israel — the real people of God, announced by the prophets as "the holy remnant." For this same reason the ties between Judaism and Christendom remained intact so long; and for this reason too, early Christendom remained faithful to the Jewish law.

Constitutionally, the Church was independent from the time of her foundation by virtue of three factors: her own **faith** (and therefore her own teaching **authority:** 1:18; chap. 15), her own **sacraments** (and therefore ordaining power to confer them) and her own **government** (legislative 15:28 ff. and judicial: 8:18-23; 5:1-11). It took several decades to become conscious of this independence. This took place not through the self-consciousness of the Mother Church, but through outside factors. Just these facts — more than her own teaching, authority, ordaining and judicial power — demonstrated her difference from Judaism: reception by Samaritans and expulsion by the great synagogue.

Characteristics

We see the four distinguishing marks of the Church, recorded in the gospels as doctrine, exemplified in the Acts.

Her **unity** in faith, brotherly love and cult become tangible in this lucid sentence of 2:42: "They devoted themselves to the apostles' teaching and fellowship, to the breaking of bread and the prayers." A short explanation seems necessary.

The "teaching of the apostles" is the catechesis,

which Luke says is well attended. We shall deal with its content when we consider apostolicity.

The sense of fellowship, especially in regard to use of earthly possessions, is constantly recorded. "The company of those who believed were of one heart and soul, and no one said that any of the things which he possessed was his own, but they had everything in common" (4:32; 2:44). "There was not a needy person among them, for as many as were possessors of lands or houses sold them, and brought the proceeds of what was sold and laid it at the apostles' feet; and distribution was made to each as any had need" (4:34 ff.; 2:45). Not all the faithful sold their possessions, nor did this happen all at once. The facts confirm this: 12:12 mentions the house of Mark's mother; that Barnabas sold a piece of ground is mentioned as if it were something special (4:36 ff.); from the story of Ananias and Saphira, it seems that the sale was a free act (5:4). One may think of a poor-box maintained by liberal contributions. It is a relative but voluntary communism restricted to the Church in Jerusalem; in other churches Paul holds collections for the Mother Church.

The third term, the breaking of the bread, is found in 2:46: ". . . and breaking bread in their homes, they partook of food with glad and generous hearts." The flat, round loaves of the Jews were not cut but broken. Hence we have the expression frequently used in the profane sense of having a meal (Lk. 9:16: feeding of the five thousand (Acts 27:35; Paul

in Malta); it is also used in the liturgical sense
of celebrating the Eucharist (Acts 2:42, 46; 20:7).
The reason for the liturgical interpretation must
have been that Jesus, before the institution of the
Eucharist, "took bread, and blessed and **broke** it,
and gave it to his apostles" (Mt. 26:26 ff., par.). The
liturgical meal was not held in the temple but in
the houses. This indicates that a proper liturgy
existed from the beginning and that the celebration
of the Eucharist formed its center. In this home-
liturgy prayer, a Christ-like procedure, was observed.
Customary oral prayers must have been based on
messianic psalms. In addition there must have been
some improvisation; the prayers of the faithful etc.
in our missal almost all date to improvisations of the
first centuries. An example is found in 4:24-30. That
those present "lifted their voices together to God"
supposes of course that there was a leader, as well
as there was in 1:24 and in worship in the synagogue.
The others presumably only answered "Amen." In
any case it is important that the primeval Christian
prayer was a community prayer, beseeching strength
in persecution as well as apostolic courage (1:14;
2:46 ff.; 4:24; 12:5); this was a realistic ecclesiastical
prayer that incorporated the requirements and in-
terests of the whole church. In those prayers one
always addressed the Father, never Christ; this can
be concluded from the texts mentioned and also
from the letters of Paul.

To all appearances therefore verse 2:42 is a summary of what took place in the assemblies of the

primitive communities: an instruction by the apostles (our epistle and gospel), a collection for the poor, celebration of the Eucharist and a number of prayers. To put it another way: the early-Christian liturgy, itself inspired by the worship of the synagogue, is in turn the prototype of our liturgy of the Mass.

Because the early Christian liturgy was characterized by the conscious participation (**koinônia**) of the whole community in the Holy Sacrifice, it is gratifying that Vatican II, in the **Constitution on the Liturgy,** evidences that it derived inspiration from this fact: it adapts the liturgy of the Mass more to the requirements of the faithful, notably by simplifying the liturgy and honorably reinstating the vernacular.

If any **one** thing has been made clear from the above, this must certainly be the unity of the nascent Church. It is a unity which grew stronger under the pressure of persecutions: a unity of cult constantly underlined by mention of their common faith and unifying brotherly love. Does Luke perhaps give us too flattering a picture? Granting this, he still does not fail — by way of contrast — to bring to light human weaknesses as shown, in the greed of Ananias and Saphira and in the friction between Greeks and Hebrews.

Besides being one, the Church in the Acts is also **universal.** The Church was this through the salvific will of her Founder; this is evident in what might be called the motto of the book (1:8). But in practice

it took years before it became conscious of this fact.
Pressure had to come from outside. Persecutions
caused the Hellenes to emigrate and thus utilize
the opportunity to spread the faith everywhere, even
though originally this took place exclusively among
the Jews. Under the impulse of the Spirit of God,
Peter goes a step further and receives the heathen
centurion Cornelius into the Church. Giving way to
this evidence of God's intervention, Jerusalem accepted the fact, without however drawing the consequences from it. Paul is the first who resolutely
takes the road to the gentiles and demolishes the
age-old barrier between Jews and gentiles. In so
doing however he maintains relations with the Mother
Church; as exemplified in Antioch, he handed over
his collections for the poor in Jerusalem. He submitted his missionary method to Jerusalem, even
though it met with opposition from countless Jewish-
Christians. At the council which resulted, the Mother
Church rewarded his services to the poor with a
decree that gentile-Christians are exempt from the
Jewish law and circumcision. This was done at the
insistence of Peter, who refers to his own experiences
with the gentile Cornelius.

The **sanctity** of the Church is guaranteed because
she has at her disposal all means of sanctification
(2:42-46; 4:32-35) and has produced in the apostles
and many of their successors true models of sanctity.
Religious enthusiasm should not remain unrecorded
as a typical feature. According to 2:46 this was a
fruit of the Eucharist; Christ came to them as food

in order to apply his death and resurrection to them. Their spiritual joy was further increased through peace of mind, through the certitude that they belonged to the new world, through seeing the miracles demonstrating divine protection, and even through the persecutions (5:41): these were regarded as fulfillment of the prophecies (4:25 ff.) and as opportunities for helping them to become more like Christ. Their joy expresses itself in prayers, ecstasies, prophecies and other charismata. A result of this is indifference for earthly possessions, altruism (**agapè**) and ideal harmony (**koinônia**).

The foundation of this unity and universality and sanctity of the Church is her **apostolicity.** Acts presents this be referring to the teaching of the apostles (2:42; 5:28), their testimony of Christ (4:2, 18; 5:21, 28, 42). This testimony concerned the earthly life of Christ — all he did and said from his baptism in the Jordan to his ascension (1:21 ff.). It has two stages: the propaganda sermon (**kerygma**) for those not yet converted and the catechesis **didachè**) for those converted. The propaganda-sermon includes three facts: (a) by raising Christ from the dead, (b) God appointed him as the Messianic King, (c) invested with salvific and judicial power. With his resurrection all the prophecies of the Old Testament are fulfilled and the messianic time has begun; hence salvific blessings — forgiveness of sins, peace of mind, supernatural life — can be obtained, on condition that one does penance and believes in Christ.

The catechesis too contains three facts. The Chris-

tian salvation message is rooted in the death and
resurrection of Christ; a little later an introduction
preceded this, namely the story of Christ's earthly
life; finally was added, by way of an informative
prologue, the history of the Old Testament insofar
as this is a preparation for Christ. Thus a synthesis
of the Christian faith was developed for the use of
the faithful. It was put in narrative form and remained in use until the Middle Ages, as is evident
from the two well known books of Augustine: **De
catechezandis rudibus** and **De doctrina Christiana.**
Under the influence of scholasticism the narrative
treatment of the catechism later fell into disuse.

Hierarchy

The beginning of the Acts introduces the apostles
as authoritative teachers: the Holy Spirit speaks for
them (2:4, 17-18; 4:8; 5:3); "teaching of the apostles"
seems to have become a standard expression. This
is of course doctrine about Christ, not doctrine about
God; Christians distinguish themselves from other
people precisely through their doctrine about Christ.
For the theological substructure of their Christology
they study the Old Testament; they search inspiration
in the blessings of Genesis, in the messianic psalms,
and especially in the suffering servant of Yahweh
(Is. 52-53).

A halo which adorns the apostles is their miracle-
power (4:7, 33). Acts 3-4 offers a beautiful illustration
of this. This text is a unit; the end, 4:22, goes back to
the beginning, 3:2; the saving name is referred to
over and over (3:6, 16; 4:7, 10, 12, 17, 18, 30).

Miracles are performed not by the apostles' own power (3:12) but by the power of Jesus (4:10); for this reason they call upon his name (3:6); the name stands for the person himself. Their faith in the person of Jesus is their strength (3:16), as it is, for that matter, for every believer (4:12; cf. v. 11). They radiate Jesus to such an extent that even their shadow brings healing (5:15).

This being filled with the Holy Spirit, in doctrine as well as by miracles, places the apostles above the crowd. Hence, religious "fear" (2:43; 5:5, 11). Not one of the authorities dares join them, but the people glorify them (5:12). It is something of cult-veneration; gifts are placed before them (4:35, 37; 5:2). In short, the primitive community is not a democracy but a theocracy, wherein the apostles act as legates and deputies of Christ. We see them preach the salvific message (1:4-8; 6:2-4), take the lead in the cenacle (1:12-26), receive the gifts (4:35 ff.). The first persecution rages against them; they conduct the election of deacons, they alone impart the Holy Spirit through the laying on of hands, they delegate Barnabas to Antioch; they decide at the council of Jerusalem. The origin of their authority is threefold: they were appointed by Christ; they were witnesses of his resurrection; they are bearers of the Holy Spirit. These three factors are organically connected.

The primacy evidently rests on Peter. He heads the list of apostles (1:13; cf. 3:1; 5:19). He decides to fill the vacant place of Judas, even though one might wonder why Jesus would not have reserved to him-

self the right of nomination for such a high office.
Peter is the spokesman of the college at Pentecost
and later before the Sanhedrin. His authority decides
the question of the reception of the gentiles, first
in the case of Cornelius, later at the council of
Jerusalem. Against his primacy, one might object that
Acts 8:14 at first sight seems to present him as no
more than an envoy of the others. But a superior
can easily undertake a mission for his inferior
brothers; thus the Jews sent their high priest Ismael
to Nero, and the Asiatic churches their bishops to
Ignatius of Antioch. When Peter accepts the mission
to go to Samaria, he does so first to honor the
Samaritans but also to be able to act with greater
authority.

By virtue of Christ's authorization, the twelve
choose their helpers. First they designate deacons
for the care of the poor in which there was some
irregularity. The people point out the candidates,
the apostles ordain them. Besides this care for the
poor, which remains their main task, they assist the
apostles by preaching and baptizing (Acts 6-8).

The Acts later mention another group of ministers,
the elders. We meet them for the first time in connection with the relief work of Antioch for Jerusalem,
where they accept the goods (11:29 ff.). Previously
the apostles had done this themselves (4:35, 37; 5:2).
But Peter disappears (12:19) and most of the others
would seem to have followed him (cf. Gal. 1:19).
It is therefore likely that the management of ecclesiastical possessions was performed in their absence

by the elders. Their power however was not restricted to this alone; they are true assistants of the
apostles. When difficulties arise in Antioch which
are submitted to the Mother Church, one can go to
them as well as to the apostles (15:2); they consult
with the apostles (15:6) results are promulgated as
decrees of the apostles and the elders (15:22 ff.;
16:4). Besides the management of ecclesiastical possessions they seem really to possess doctrinal power,
though dependent on the apostles. They form a
permanent council; when Paul visits Jerusalem ten
years later for the last time, he finds James there,
along with the council of elders (21:18).

The Acts are silent about the origin of this office
in Jerusalem. But we see Paul and Barnabas appointing elders, with the laying on of hands and prayer,
during their first missionary journey in the newly
founded community (14:22). These elders had to
preside at liturgical assemblies, celebrate the breaking of bread, lead the flock — in a word "rule" the
community (20:28). The two missionaries take the
primeval community as an example of this. We may
conclude that the elders are persons upon whom
the apostles conferred the sacerdotal dignity to care
for the spiritual and temporal welfare of the communities. As the Jewish elders in Jerusalem assisted
the high priest, so the Christian elders are counsellors
of the head of the community. There is nevertheless
an essential difference. Among the early Jews the
elders were not priests; in Jerusalem itself the group
of **presbyteroi** (elders) is clearly distinguished from the

archiereis, who only belong to the priest families. In the Christian communities the elders are chosen to assist the apostles and their successors in pastoral work and sacred services, and are therefore invested with sacerdotal dignity. Like the deacons, the elders or presbyters have a hierarchical origin. They are not simply representatives or delegates of the people; they are called by the apostles, from whom they receive their appointment and power.

Sacraments

As a visible and hierarchical society the Church has as her task the sanctification of souls, through bringing them to Christ, the one indispensable principle of all sanctification (4:11 ff.; 20:21). Justification does not occur through direct infusion of the Holy Spirit, but through ceremonies which we call **sacraments.** The Acts mention four.

The only entrance to the Church is baptism (2:37 ff.; 8:12 ff., 36 ff.). Exceptional callings do not obviate this: Paul and the centurion Cornelius are also baptized (20:10, 16; 10:47). "Baptizing in the name of Jesus" (2:28 etc.), mentioned several times, means simply Christian baptism in contrast to the baptism of John (19:3-5). It says nothing of the baptism formula, which was Trinitarian from the first century, as can be concluded from the equalization of "baptizing in the name of the Lord" with baptizing "in the name of the Father and the Son and the Holy Spirit" in Didachè 9:5 and 7:1-3.

Confirmation is essentially different from baptism,

as is witnessed in Samaria and Ephesus (8:16; 19:5 ff.). In the latter case the Spirit is imparted through laying on of hands and prayer. The accompanying prayer always defines the meaning of the laying on of hands (deacons 6:6; missionaries 13:3; the sick 28:8). It is also evident from both examples that those confirmed were already baptized and that the administration of confirmation itself was reserved to the highest leaders.

The ordination sacrament too took place through the laying on of hands with prayer: deacons in 6:6; priests (**presbyteroi**) 14:23. Consecration of bishops is not recorded. All these rites give the impression that they are permanent; they are not gifts of grace for a special time, but treasures entrusted to the Church for the spiritual welfare of all her members. All come from Christ. By baptism, breaking of bread, and laying on of hands the apostles act according to the wishes of the Master. Confirmation answers to the design of the risen Christ; it brought the Spirit of Pentecost to the newly baptized; Jesus' wish that the apostles remain in the cenacle to await the Spirit was reason enough for them to pass him on to all the faithful. Forgiveness of sin in Acts is brought about only through baptism. Nevertheless it is obvious that the apostolic powers concerning pardon are not limited only to the baptism rite; this naturally takes place only once. That marriage and extreme unction are not mentioned in these historical chapters, need not be a surprise.

The Holy Spirit

At his departure Jesus did not not want to leave his disciples orphans. He sent them his Spirit as "Paraclete," as John calls him — that is, as protector and helper rather than comforter. His task is not just to safeguard the apostles from sadness, but very positively to assist and strengthen them to be witnesses for Christ. Thus the **Spiritus Paraclitus** leads the disciples into perfect truth. Because Jesus himself is the truth, it means that the Spirit gives them perfect insight into the revelation about Jesus and the ability to preach him to the world. The Spirit extends through them, in time and space, the work of redemption begun by Christ. The Spirit who formerly worked in the historical person of Jesus, and through him in the Palestine of those days, works henceforth through the apostolic witnesses in the whole world. In this new way the same power is at work and the same salvation offered (1:8).

Communication of the Spirit calls the Church into existence. The new era, which dawns with Christ's entering into glory, is as much the time of the Spirit as the time of the Church. Without the Church the Spirit would be a power without a sphere of action; without Spirit the Church would be a body without a soul. Since the first Pentecost, Spirit and Church are inseparably joined.

The Spirit governs the Church and works in and through her. As has often been noted, the principal figure in the book of the Acts is not Peter, nor Paul, but the Spirit who extends the Church and confirms her (9:31), who inspires the decisions necessary to maintain her unity (15:28), who conducts the apostles and their assistants on their mission journeys (4:8; 6:10; 8:29; 10:19; 13:2; 20:24), who institutes necessary offices in the Church (6:6; 20:28), who provides prophetic warnings (11:28; 21:4-11).

It is striking how, in the Acts, the Spirit operates almost exclusively on charismatic ground; this means that he influences certain persons for the good of the whole Church. This particular influence is directed to the establishment and extension of the Church (horizontal); one detects little in the Acts of an actual sanctifying influence upon individuals (vertical).

Of the charismata in strict sense we should mention especially the gift of tongues. The Acts often mention this, as at Pentecost, with Cornelius and company (10:46), with the disciples of John in Ephesus (19:6) and possibly also with the Samaritans (8:15-18). Another charism is prophecy, which sometimes unveils a future event (Agabus in 11:28; unknown persons in 21:11 ff.); usually it gives a deeper insight into the Gospel. In Antioch the prophets are therefore mentioned with the teachers (13:1); furthermore, Judas and Silas and the four daughters of Philip are mentioned as such (15:32; 21:9).

Some Protestants see a contradiction between the charismatic office and a more juridically orientated ecclesiastical organization. Regulated organs of government would have come into existence only when the charismatic functions gradually were quenched and disappeared. We do not think this is correct. Quite the contrary: both kinds of functionaries, however much they differ, do not form clearly distinct, much less opposing, groups. One can detect in Paul an endeavor to stabilize the three most important charismata — of apostles, prophet and teacher — (which suppose a certain specialization and a certain duration) so that the man and his office become almost one. With or without special spiritual powers these functionaries have had their own terrain allocated. Charismatic functions are much less represented in Jerusalem than in hellenistic Christendom. There — in Jerusalem — government from the beginning resided in the apostles.

Charismatic in a broader sense is the influence of the Spirit wherever he equips preachers and rulers of the Church with extraordinary power. Thus with Peter (2:33; 4:8; 10:9), Stephen (6:10), Philip (8:29), Paul (13:9; 16:6 ff.) etc. Here also we remain on charismatic terrain directed to establishment and extension of the Church, and not to the sanctification of souls.

Sanctification of souls through the Spirit remains entirely in the background in Luke. Indeed Peter promises the Spirit to all who let themselves be baptized (2:38), gentiles not excluded (2:39); but it still is not clear whether the Spirit is directly imparted through baptism and, still less clear, what he in fact does. We hear elsewhere that the Spirit comes only through the laying on of hands (8:17; 19:6); speaking with tongues is recorded solely as a result of his coming (10:45; 19:6). Nowhere therefore is he directly connected with sanctification of souls, as he so splendidly is in Paul. Would this perhaps not indicate the archaic character of the theology of the Acts, an older phase of theology than is found in Paul? Naturally one could assert that the historian Luke did not concern himself with inner sanctification while Paul, the theologian, did; but then the less-developed theology of Acts could be credited to the author and not to the primeval community. But let us not be mistaken! As we have seen, Luke speaks indeed of the sanctity of the primeval community (2:42-47; 4; 32; 5:12 ff.) and, what is most striking, he does not attribute this sanctity to the Holy Spirit! In any case, however one prefers to explain it, the fact is that the Acts — in contrast with the letters of Paul — represent the Spirit not as the operator of personal sanctity, of religious and moral life in the primeval community, but exclusively as a power emanating from God, which by propulsive force and inspiration and enlightenment confirms and extends the Kingdom of God.

4

OUTWARD APPEARANCE OF THE CHURCH IN PAUL

Her names

It is obvious that Paul, who regards the Church as heir of Israel, recalled the traditional Old Testament metaphors to designate the Church. As we know, these represent the chosen people now as a **vineyard** jealously guarded and carefully kept by God (Is. 5:2-7), now as a **vine** of unlimited growing-power transplanted to Canaan (Ps. 80:9-12). The first figure recurs in the synoptics, the second in John. Paul however makes use of both, but alters them: from the vineyard he makes a field (1 Cor. 3:6-9), from the vine an olive tree (cf. Jer. 11:16; Hos. 14:7) — this lends itself more easily to the grafting process (Rom. 11:16-24). The allegory is clear: the "holy root" are the patriarchs; the olive tree — like the remnant of Israel — is the Church; her members are the branches, whether her own (Jewish-Christians) or graftings produced upon her (gentile-Christians). Unbelief snaps off old branches, belief produces new graftings; but the broken off branches can always hope for re-union, while the graftings in their turn must always fear they may be torn off.

Furthermore, Israel was regarded as a **house**, as **kingdom,** as **people,** of which Yahweh was father, king, God. As heir of the synagogue the Church will take over these titles, though not without modification. Thus "house of God" for Paul means a family rather than a building, though the latter is not absent; this then easily proceeds to the figure of a temple with foundation and cornerstone (Eph. 2: 19-21), in which God dwells (2 Cor. 6:16). "Kingdom of God" too, an ordinary figure in the synoptics, receives from Paul a more eschatological, application in "inherit the Kingdom of God" (1 Cor. 6:9 ff.; 15:50; Gal. 5:21; Eph. 5:5). "People of God" is for him the Church as cited in Old Testament quotations; the Palestinian figure "flock" does not appear in Paul.

The chosen people's title of honor was **daughter** and **bride** of Yahweh. In the new salvific order the title "Son" gets a deeper sense; from collective it becomes individual, so that the community itself rather than her separate members are called "Children of God." Actually the name "bride" should have followed the same process. But the marriage metaphor, common with the old prophets, is scarce in the New Testament. John recalls it in his wedding feast of the Lamb (Rev. 21:6-9; 22:17), Paul, does so when as friend of the bridegroom he wants to present to his Master a pure bride (2 Cor. 11:2), and especially when he calls Christian marriage a great mystery "in connection with Christ and his Church" (Eph. 5:22-33).

Finally there is one figure that enjoys the pre-dilection of the apostle: the Church as **the body of Christ.** This does not appear anywhere else in the Bible. The vine and the branches of John 15 is the Palestinian parallel to Paul's Hellenistic figure of body and limbs. The Apostle himself has at his disposal another figure — that of the temple with Christ as cornerstone; he is not the only one, for one finds this figure of the temple also in 1 Pet. 2:4-6. In Paul, who so easily moves from one metaphor to another (Eph. 2:19-22: house, kingdom, building, temple), the figure of the temple is often mixed with others. He sees the faithful at the same time "rooted in Christ and founded upon Christ" (Col. 2:6); he sees Jews and gentiles received in the one new "man," after the "barrier" has been taken down (Eph. 2:14 ff.); he sees growth taking place in the whole body unto the "building up" of self in love (Eph. 4:16). This does not alter his preference for the Church as body. We will speak of this later.

The preference of Vatican II is the title "People of God" (Nos. 9-17). Without overlooking the figure of the "Mystical Body" — quite the contrary — and without neglecting the other metaphors in Holy Scripture (they all illuminate a particular aspect of the Church), the Council especially chose the metaphor of the "People of God." It did this because this figure expresses most embracing aspects and, above all, aspects most needed in our time. To begin with, it makes clear that the Church does not pri-marily consist of a series of religious truths, laws and ceremonies, it is rather a community of living men: it is a people. Further, the People of God means, that these people make history, develop, have-not-yet-arrived and therefore need and deserve time to grow, to be on-the-way, to seek and to grope. God has a salvific plan with and for men. He addresses man and calls him to grow through and in him toward his final perfection. Finally there are in a people on-the-way certain possible gradations; we can find room for different Churches, and even see the immense throng of non-Christians within the perspective of salvation (cf. Nos. 13-17).

This description of the Church as a dynamic reality seems to me scripturally most strongly founded in the prefigurations of the people of God in the Old Covenant. The letter to the Hebrews indicates this parallel. The purpose of this letter to the Jewish converts is that, in spite of all difficulties, they must persevere in faith in Jesus Christ. The starting point is God's salvific plan to lead humanity into his intimacy. The promise to Abraham alludes to this. This was partially fulfilled for the people of Israel when they took possession of the promised land; for us, the new people of God, it is to be completely fulfilled in the homeland of heaven: the author demonstrates this in his digression about the Remnant (chaps. 3 and 4).

To reach this goal we must remain firm in the faith. Faith is unwavering trust in God who is faithful and unswerving in his resolution. In the struggles and trials of life the faithful must remain as loyal as a child who relies entirely on the guidance of his father. This we do, not as individuals, but as members of the great people of God who, like the wandering people of Moses, are on the way as a community. A fatal danger threatens when one cuts himself from the caravan to go his own way. This is equal to apostasy — being cut off from the people of God as bearer of God's promise. Such a one misses the revelation, the guidance of the shepherd, every guarantee of mediation.

The metaphor of nomads and pilgrims is not sufficient for Christendom; the people of God is at the same time a community with a cult, as were the people of Israel in the desert. If faith directs the course of life, cult leads it to God. The journey aims not so much at a place of rest, as at a temple: the new people of God are going up to a sanctuary (predicted in Is. 2:2 ff.). This sacred ascending is expressed by the Old Testament term for the ascending of the priest to the temple and altar (sixteen times **eiserchomai,** seven times **proserchomai** in this Epistle). The people of God is on the way to the eschaton — the Holy of Holies.

John also constantly alludes to this new Exodus (Jn. 3:14; 6:32 ff.; 7:37 ff.; 8:12); this is his way of introducing the new people of God. He does this still more explicitly in his biblical figures of bride (3:29), flock (10:1-16) and branches of the vine (15:1-17). 1 Pet. 2:9 ff. indicates the same.

Her characteristics

If this series of constantly changing figures —
Kingdom of God, people of God, family of God,
God's house or temple, God's field, the olive tree with
holy root and trunk, — suggests one thing, this certainly is the **unity of the Church.** This is most clear
in the metaphor, the body of Christ.

Since there is only one Christ, there can be only
one mystical body. "For as many of you as were
baptized into Christ, have put on Christ. There
is neither Jew nor Greek, there is neither slave
nor free, there is neither male nor female: for
you are all one in Christ Jesus" (Gal. 3:27 ff.). When
Paul wants to put an end to the clique-spirit in
Corinth, he exclaims: "Is Christ divided?" (1 Cor.
1:13). To divide the Church is the same as to divide
Christ himself. One may therefore never break away
from him who is the head; never listen to those
who falsify the faith (Col. 2:18 ff.), whose supporters
are "children, tossed to and fro and carried about
with every wind of doctrine, by the cunning of men
by their craftiness in deceitful wiles" (Eph. 4:14).

The most beautiful praise of unity is this passage
from Ephesians: "Eager to maintain the unity of the
Spirit in the bond of peace. There is one body and
one Spirit, just as you were called to the one hope, that
belongs to your call, one Lord, one faith, one baptism. One God and Father of us all, who is above
all and through all and in all" (Eph. 4:3-6).

Seven elements — three inner, three external, and

one co-ordinating contribute to the unity of the Church. One is her material principle, because she is but one body; one is her formal principle, because she is animated by the same Spirit; one is her object: eternal happiness. She is one also in her leadership, one through her common confession of faith and one through her rite of baptism, which assures her existence and expansion. The last motive of her unity is her origin: "One God and Father of us all" (cf. Eph. 3:15).

One can better understand, in view of this enthusiastic proclamation of unity, why Paul warns so emphatically against the rising gnosticism; and one more easily understands the importance of monarchical rule, already perceptible in early Christendom and later more sharply outlined in the episcopate. To breach the unity of faith through heresy and schism will always be regarded as an inadmissable rending of the cloak without seam.

Another attribute of the Church is her **universality.** This was announced by the Old Testament, for the nations shall join with Israel (Is. 2:2-4; Mich. 4:1-5); they shall share in the blessing promised to Abraham (Jer. 4:2; cf. Gen. 12:3 and 18:22) and in the covenant of which the mysterious Servant of Yahweh will be the mediator (Is. 42:6). Nowhere in the New Testament has this universality been brought to light so forcibly as by him who rightly is called the "apostle of the gentiles." During his three missionary journeys in the years 45-57 A.D. he founded Christian communities everywhere and then set forth for Rome and Spain. If no one less than Christ himself had given the Church through his mission-command a universal destination, Paul would have been required to make this universality a fact: more than anyone else he enabled the Church to take into her bosom innumerable cities, provinces and nations. With pride he could testify: "Christ we proclaim; warning every man and teaching every man in wisdom, that we may present every man mature in Christ" (Col. 1:28). Gentiles, despised till then, "separated from Christ, alienated and strangers to the covenants of promise, having no hope and without God in the world" are now amalgamated with the chosen ones into a new people. They are no longer "Strangers and sojourners," but as full-fledged members of the Church they are from now on "fellow citizens with the saints and members of the household of God" (Eph. 2:11 ff.).

The originality of Paul consists precisely in this: he concludes the unity and universality from his concept of the Church itself. As he sees her, the Church is in essence universal; she excludes everything contrary to unity and universality, through bridging over all national, social and personal differences on the religious plane. She does this by pouring into all her members a communal stream of life and inexhaustible energy. "Here there cannot be Greek and Jew, circumcised and uncircumcised, barbarian, Scythian, slave, free man, but Christ is all, and in all" (Col. 3:11; cf. Gal. 3:26-28). Differences of race, upbringing, status and even sex are removed by becoming a child of God. No one is excluded from this one great Christian family; even the Scythians, then regarded as the most barbaric race, were admitted.

It was not enough to spread the Gospel everywhere (Rom. 10:18); one must remove the obstacles to complete integration of the heterogeneous elements. The main obstacle was Jewish particularism. The Jewish theocracy had absolutely no pretensions of becoming a world religion, for the loss of her nationalistic tendencies would have been an abandoning of her privileged status (cf. Rom. 9:4). She would admit new members, but by classifying them she made perfectly clear that she did not in the least intend to make humanity into one great religious family. The law of Moses, once the guardian of the monotheistic faith of the Jews, kept them in fatal isolation. If Jesus Christ willed to assure unity and universality for his Church, then it was necessary that he first demolish this barrier. For that reason he nailed to the cross the superannuated writings which prevented the union of the nations (Col. 2:14). With this he opened wide the gates for the new salvific order for all nations which previously had remained separated; all men become with the same title fellow-citizens of the same kingdom and members of the same family. United with one another and with God, all men have finally become one in Christ in one great mystical family (Eph. 2:14-19; cf. Col. 1:20-22).

Paul promulgated the abolition of the old Law with so much emphasis that his adversaries called him an apostate and obstructed him on all his journeys. This was a blind prejudice which could not grasp the complexity of Paul's viewpoint. He regarded the law itself as good; it came from God and was supposed to lead to God. Its weak spot was that it was light without power. Human covetousness made it a stumbling block; in its impotence it had no remedy against this covetousness (Rom. 7:7-25). As an instrument of sin Paul classifies it among our adversaries and condemns it in at least six texts (Rom. 3:20; 4:15; 5:20; 7:8; 1 Cor. 15:56; Gal. 3:19). This is the negative aspect of the Law, for which men themselves were guilty. The positive aspect which God intended lies in its educative character. It gave Israel a line of conduct which was to guard it against pagan depravity; it strengthened the notion of sin; it was meant to convince Israel more and more of its own inadequacy to better prepare it for the redemption (Gal. 3:22-24). From all this it is evident that the Law was meant to be temporary. As a disciplinary code it led ignorant humanity to Christ; now that he has come, this task is done: the old salvation order must make room for the new, the Law for grace, the letter for the Spirit.

Universal salvation thus broke a nationalistic system. Paul could therefore announce that justification results not from observance of the Law but from acceptance of the Gospel. To the Galatians and Romans he protests against the pharisaic view that justification was the fruit of human effort. True justification is a gift of God, through pure mercy and through Christ's merits. Paul is convinced that he can serve universality of salvation better by insisting on God's absolute freedom to decide whom he will call and how he will grant his gifts to those who are called. This clarifies the fact that justification is unmerited; this, for the gentiles who are so poor in good works, is considered good fortune. Inadvertence to this truth was fatal for the Jews; their pride in their pretended works precluded the need of a mediator: they did not feel themselves drawn to a Messiah who demanded only faith (Rom. 9:30; 10:4). In the final analysis therefore it is our own wretchedness which makes us incapable of the supernatural; and it is God's grace that has sent Christ to redeem us from sin and to shower upon us various benefits. This is indeed the most profound foundation for salvific universality in Paul.

One and universal in essence, the Church is also **apostolic.** Paul writes to the Ephesians: "You are built upon the foundation of the apostles and prophets, Christ Jesus himself being the cornerstone," (Eph. 2:20). For this building, of which Christ is the cornerstone and the faithful the living stones, the foundation has to be of the same nature and therefore must consist of persons. Are the prophets here mentioned those of the Old or of the New Testament? With most other commentators we hold they pertain to the latter; they are mentioned after the apostles and under the same definite article, which seems to place them in the same category (cf. Eph. 3:5 and 4:11).

That finally **sanctity** is also an essential attribute of the Church, does not stand out anywhere as well as in Eph. 5:25-27: "Husbands, love your wives, as Christ loved the Church and gave himself up for her, that he might sanctify her, having cleansed her by the washing of water with the word, that he might present the Church to himself in splendor, without spot or wrinkle or any such thing, that she might be holy and without blemish."

This remarkable text is part of an instruction about the duties of Christian newly-weds (epistle of the wedding mass). Christ and his Church are the model for husband and wife. The wife ought to follow her husband as the Church follows Christ; the husband must love his wife as Christ loves the Church.

How this love of Christ towers above any possible human love! It is unmerited: Christ loved the Church not because she was beautiful, but he made her beautiful in order to love her. It is an unselfish love which drove him to death for her. It is a noble love which made him seek for his beloved the greatest happiness: "He gave himself up for her that he might sanctify her." The beauty of the Church is sketched in delicate strokes in which the veiled comparison with a bride enhances the charm. First the baptism-bath, accompanied with sacramental words, cleansed the Church from every stain. But the solicitude of

the divine lover did not restrict himself to the for-
giving of sins. He wants a radiant bride. She must
not only be beautiful inwardly, but must radiate her
beauty outwardly, so that she can arouse the admira-
tion of angels and men.

A husband is not always able to give his wife
the beauty which nature has withheld. Christ can
do that. No stain may deface his bride, no wrinkle
which might suggest fatigue or old age. Eternal
youth and strength must emanate from her. This
portrait, so characteristic in its conciseness, should
be sufficient to show us the divine beauty of the
Church through its conformity with human beauty.
But the apostle goes a step further by specifying the
intention of the Savior: he loved the Church, gave
himself up for her, cleansed her through baptism
and exalted her as bride "that she might be holy
and without blemish." Holy means consecrated to
God. The Church is consecrated to Christ, is his
own as bride is to bridegroom; as a result of this
intimacy she is invested with grace, gifts and virtues.
In Paul's view the cohabitation of the spouses is a
great mystery" (v. 32), because it has the union
Christ-Church as model and ideal. If "man shall leave
his father and mother and be joined to his wife, and
the two shall become one" (v. 31), how much more
true is this of Christ and the Church! If a human
married couple have everything in common, does not
the Church see herself enriched and adorned with
all the treasures of Christ who is sanctity itself? The
second term "without blemish" emphasizes once

again the perfection expressed by the preceding term. This ideal will naturally be realized only in heaven. Nevertheless on earth the Church will always possess the luster of sanctity which will delight her Bridegroom and distinguish her for men as his chosen beloved.

Christians who are called, baptized and are members of Christ's body are usually called "saints" by the apostle — a usage unknown in the gospels. Christian sanctity means withdrawal from the profane and consecration to God, with accent on the latter: consecration is a partaking in sanctity itself. To do honor to this name the Christian is bound to practice virtues, the germ of which was deposited in him through baptism. The human element in these "saints" so often annoys us — it is evident from 1 Cor. that it was no different in Paul's time! — but according to his doctrine the enormous power of God is nevertheless at work in them (Eph. 1:19; 3:16, 20; 6:10) and this guarantees their sanctity.

Her government

All the communities founded by Paul were directly dependent on him. "The care of all the Churches" rested indeed on him (2 Cor. 11:28). It is possible that this centralization delayed for a time the rise of a monarchical episcopate, but it was necessary at the outset to assure the mutual unity of the Churches and to cope with eventual schisms. The hellenistic churches sparkled with life and activity. This is especially true in Corinth. There were factions where one agreed with Paul, another with Apollo; even the celebration of the Eucharist did not remain free from a clique-spirit. They even went to court and before pagan judges! In spite of the pessimistic aspects, one is nevertheless caught by the new ideals: married people seek separation in order to live in continence, young girls wish to live in perfect chastity, numerous spiritual gifts bring the faithful to ecstasy. From a point of view of dogma the new faith raises many problems. Is it permissable to eat meat which had been offered to idols? Everyone believes in Christ's resurrection, but will the departed Christians also rise? What happens to the buried body? Some let themselves be baptized once more on behalf of unbaptized departed. Who is going to bring order in all these aberrations? Who is going to guide these grown children? And according to what rules?

The first authoritative norm is **tradition.** Since this dates to Christ himself no one is allowed to tamper with it (2 Thess. 3:6; Phil. 4:9). The apostle designates as "tradition" religious truths like Christ's death and resurrection, the Eucharist, etc. (1 Cor. 15:23 ff.); he includes ecclesiastical practices (1 Cor. 11:16; 14:33 ff.). On occasion he takes principles known to all as a starting point in order to solve difficulties submitted to him, to formulate religious truths or to draw up disciplinary rules, as, for example, regarding married life (1 Cor. 7:10-25), conduct of women in the liturgical assemblies (11:2-16), the order to be observed in the celebration of the Eucharist, etc. In short, the tradition concept, a complex of articles of faith and directions which go

back to Christ and thus concern all churches, abounds
in all the letters of Paul. Especially in the pastoral
letters he keeps insisting that Titus and Timothy
should remain faithful to the traditional doctrine,
to keep this as an inviolable legacy (1 Tim. 6:20 ff.;
2 Tim. 2:1 ff.) and to protect it against innovations.

To pass on the tradition, to explain and to amplify
why there necessarily must be a living and infallible
authority, we look to **the apostle himself.** His whole
letter to the Galatians and long chapters in his second
letter to the Corinthians are a protest against any
mutilation of the gospel he has preached. Paul can
and must exact unconditional belief in his preaching
because he knows himself to be a reliable link in
the tradition (Gal. 1:8; 1 Cor. 4:1-2, 17). He knows
he is an ambassador of Christ and demands that his
preaching be taken for what it is: the word of God
(2 Cor. 10:4-5). He speaks with no less authority to
the Romans whom he had not converted, as well as
to the Galatians and Corinthians for whom he is a
spiritual father. Nothing is more alien to Paul
than "private interpretation."

With his teaching authority he also possesses full
adminstrative power: he settles what should be the
attitude in regard to the pagan courts of law, the
position of women in the Church, the Eucharistic
assemblies, the use of spiritual gifts, the married life,
the rights of virgins, the collections. Administrative
power also includes power to punish (1 Cor. 4:21).
The strikers of Thessalonica await the return of
Christ. At first he is gentle with them by pointing

out to them that, after all, he himself works (2 Thess. 3:6-12); he asks the brethren to deal gently with them (v. 15). But if the strikers "refuse to obey what we say in this letter" then refuse to have anything to do with them (v. 14); expulsion will bring them to their senses. For a more serious outrage expulsion takes on terrible proportions: Paul orders the Corinthians to publicly expose the incestuous aggressor who violated them: if this is of no avail, they should leave him to satan, who may, through bodily torments, bring him to repentance (1 Cor. 5:1-5). He excommunicated Hymenaeus and Alexander for heresy (1 Tim. 1:20). He prescribes that Titus and Timothy use as a general rule the procedure which he himself always applied. Establish the fact of guilt in the presence of two or three witnesses; then proceed to the warning, first privately, later in public (1 Tim. 5:19-21; Tit. 3:10 ff.); finally, break the obstinacy by excommunication (Tit. 3:10). This is also a tradition which goes back to Christ (Mt. 18:15-17).

From this strong centralization of authority one may not however deduce that the Pauline communities were without **local leaders.** We have seen how Paul appointed elders in every community on his first missionary journey (Acts 14:23). With this appointment an ordination was definitely intended; as far as one can go back in salvation history, every ordination was accompanied by "fasting and prayer." That such an ordination is mentioned only once in the Acts is entirely in line with Luke's narrative fashion;

he dislikes repetition. Of all the sermons of Paul, he gives only two: one for a Jewish and one for a gentile audience (Acts 13 and 17); these were evidently meant to be sermon guides. One must therefore suppose that Paul administered ordinations in all his other communities. There is no need to be surprised therefore that Luke later mentions the elders of Ephesus (Acts 20:17) without previously having mentioned their appointment. Paul gives these elders his last instructions. The same persons, one observes, are first called **presbyteri** (v. 17) and later **episcopi** (v. 28). Their task is to "tend" the flock — the same term with which Christ appointed Peter as chief shepherd. Paul doubtlessly assigned them, but their appointment is from God: "the Holy Spirit has appointed you as **episcopi** to rule God's Church."

In Thessalonica Paul urges the brethren to have respect for their "leaders." We do not know whether these persons accepted this office spontaneously or were appointed by the apostle; in any case he acknowledges them in this function and points to their duties: "admonish the idle, encourage the faint-hearted, help the weak, be patient with them all" (1 Thess. 5:12-14).

In Philippi the bishops and deacons receive a special greeting from the Apostle (Phil. 1:1). In the same letter Paul praises Epaphroditus, who had sent him provisions in the name of the Philippians and whom he calls "my brother, and fellow worker and fellow soldier" (2:25). These titles, as well as the fact that the Philippians made him their confidant, make it obvious that he is deferred to as the head of the community. Had he also possessed ordination over and above this administrative position, then we would here have the first example of the monarchical episcopate. The same holds for Epaphras of Colossae (Col. 1:7; 4:2). Nevertheless one perceives how much theorizing is hidden here.

Some years later, about 65-66, the pastoral letters speak of deacons and **presbyteri-episcopi** as of two classes of clergy which regularly appear (1 Tim. 3:1-13; 5:19-20; Tit. 1:5-9). As in Acts 20:17 and 28, the names **presbyter** and **episcopus** are synonymous and interchangeable (cf. Tit. 1:5, **presbyter;** 1:7, **episcopus**). Moreover, the same qualifications are required of both. Catholic interpreters are agreed today that the New Testament has no specific names to express the distinction between priest and bishop. The qualities of these **presbyteri-episcopi** are actually no different from those every good Christian should possess: monogamy and a certain degree of knowledge; a great deal more is required of Titus and Timothy (1 Tim. 2:6-16; 6:11-16 etc.). In short, everything points to simple priests in the **presbyteri-episcopi** of the pastoral letters.

Only Titus and Timothy charged with the ordination of deacons and priests (1 Tim. 3:8-10; 5:19-22; Tit. 1:5-7), possess the power of bishops in the modern sense. They represent the apostle in a definite area and for a specific time (2 Tim. 4:13,

21; Tit. 3:12). They are travelling rather than resi-
dent bishops — but that is immaterial.

Thus we find in the churches of Paul, as well as
in those of Jerusalem, three hierarchical degrees:
deacon, priests (**presbyteri** or **episcopi**) and bishops
who can ordain and have a more extensive juridical
power, as Titus and Timothy; and over them is
Paul himself. One can readily foresee that after the
death of the apostles these former understudies will
personally continue on in the perennial exercise of
administration.

Her celibate clergy

Let us now discuss the present-day crisis of cler-
ical celibacy. Nowhere does Scripture postulate a
compelling bond between office and celibacy; it
does point however to the messianic meaning of continence for the sake of the Kingdom of God. In the
original apostolic era of the Church, functionaries
received as their "apostolic rule of life," the precept
that they were not to remarry after the death of
their wife (1 Tim. 3:2 and Tit. 1:6 for the **episcopi-
presbyteri;** 1 Tim. 3:12 for the deacons). Since the
functionaries of that time were normally already
married (practically everyone at the time was married before his twentieth year), this apostolic rule
of life implied a strong suggestion not to marry
after the reception of an important office; this was
sanctioned for the Eastern and Latin Church at the
Council of Nicea.

As to this background, one can make a distinction,

drawn from the Bible, between actual celibacy (not marrying) and continence (which Paul recommends also for the married); but for celibacy, of which little explicit is to be found, one can and must turn also to the "continence" texts. Besides, one should remember that the old Church order (Pastoral letters) has **subordinate** ecclesiastical offices in view, namely the **episcopi-presbyteri** (leaders of the local churches) and deacons; they are not allowed to remarry. Nothing is said directly of the apostles themselves or of Timothy and Titus, their helpers. The quote "leave all things and follow Christ," although intended for all Christians, was obviously understood by the apostles and the disciples of Christ in the stricter sense as a life-exemplar for themselves.

Of the synoptic gospels, Matthew and Mark had written that he who wants to be Christ's disciple (Christian) has to leave everything: "house or brothers, or sisters or mother or father or children or lands" (Mt. 19:29; Mk. 10:28-29), — in other words, patriarchical family along with its goods and chattels. Luke on the other hand leaves "lands" out, but adds "or wife" (18:29), obviously in connection with a previous text (Lk. 14:25-26). The insertion may simply mean a rounding off of the complete metaphor of the family without further implications. But, as a clear secondary text, he may also point to a notion, strong in the apostolic church, of "leaving the wife" for the sake of the Kingdom of God; Luke mentions "house and wife" **first** on the list. The

radical word — "leave" is weakened to "hate"; we
say "weakened,": to a Semite "hate" means, in such
a context, "to love less." The purpose therefore is to
love God above all things. These texts say nothing directly about celibacy, but they may well signify Paul's
preference for continence and, in view of the spirit
of the time, they might be so understood by the
first generation. Following generations in any case
have understood it in this way; so also has their
ecclesiastical leader.

5

THE CHURCH IN HER
LIFE OF GRACE IN PAUL

God's eternal salvific plan

To find the origin of the life of grace we must go back to **the eternal salvation-plan of God.** Paul mentions this many times; he uses the word "mystery" (1 Cor. 2:7-10; Rom. 16:25 ff.; Col. 1:25-27; Eph. 1:9 ff.; 3:3-6; 3:8 ff.). He calls it this, not for its incomprehensibility, but because it was concealed in God before it was revealed to us. With this designation the apostle remains faithful to the notion of "mystery" current in the apocalyptic (idea) of late Judaism; mysteries are events of the end time fixed by God but remaining hidden until they are fulfilled at the time appointed by him, and thus brought to light (Wisd. 2:22; 6:22; Dan. 2:18; 27-30 and the apocrypha, especially Enoch). Such mystery has two characteristics a hidden content, and reservation for the end time. Hence Paul can say of the salvific mystery that it "was kept secret for long ages" and "is now disclosed" (Rom. 16:25; Col. 1:26; Eph. 3:5, 9-10) in the central event of salvation history, the act of redemption which God effected in Christ Jesus.

What then is the content of this "mystery" of which Paul always speaks and which is not always clear? Fortunately, a description is given in Eph. 3:6: "that the gentiles are fellow heirs, members of the same body, and partakers of the promise in Christ Jesus through the gospel." The mystery has thus become a fact: the gentiles share with the Jews in the salvation of Christ's Church.

This mystery is rich in shades of meaning; as one or other aspect is exposed, the mystery is given different appellations. The first one is "mystery of Christ" or "Christ-mystery" (Eph. 3:4; Col. 4:3). Why? Because the eschatological fact, described as a mystery, was executed in Jesus Christ: he abolished the law through his redemptive death and thus demolished the dividing wall of hostility between Jews and gentiles. By one and the same act he reconciled both parties with God and brought them together into the one great body which is animated by God (Eph. 2:13-18). He who heralded peace (Eph. 2:17) also brought it (Eph. 2:14a). By extension, this mystery of Christ assumes world proportions: "to unite all things in him" (Eph. 1:9-10). The second appellation is "mystery of God" (Col. 2:2), insofar as the eternal decree comes from God (Eph. 1:9, 3:11), and now has been realized through him. In connection with the extension of God's salvific plan for the whole world, Paul can speak of "the unsearchable riches" and of "the riches of the glory" (Eph. 3:8; Col. 1:27), because God therein reveals the infinite love with which he leads salvation history to its goal.

Once realized, the mystery still had to be revealed in order to penetrate the knowledge of all men. This is the meaning of the act of redemption: Christ, the peace of Jews and gentiles, their amalgamation in the Church, their access to the Father in the same Spirit (Eph. 2:13-18) could be revealed only by the Spirit, after Pentecost. This happened "to his holy apostles and prophets" (Eph. 3:5), to the saints to whom God chose to make known the mystery (Col. 1:26), and especially to Paul, to whom he had given the grace to preach it to the gentiles (Eph. 3:2, 8). After that it acquired still a third appellation: "the mystery of the Gospel" (Eph. 6:19).

Act of redemption

Since the salvific plan emanated from God, he also took the initiative in its realization. For this reason he sent his own Son to redeem us (Gal. 4:4 ff.; Eph. 2:4-6).

To be able to expiate our guilt, the emissary must be able to represent us — in other words, to become one of us. The idea of solidarity between Redeemer and redeemed recurs again and again. "Christ is born of woman, born under the law" (Gal. 4:4 ff.); "Christ redeemed us from the curse of the law, having become a curse for us on the tree" (Gal. 3:13); "for our sake he made him to be sin, who knew no sin . . ." (2 Cor. 5:21); "God sent his own Son in the likeness of sinful flesh" (Rom. 8:3).

By virtue of this solidarity Christ is the head of redeemed humanity. The history of mankind for

Paul is rooted in the persons of both its progenitors:
Adam and Jesus Christ. Humanity falls and rises
in its representative. Pauline theology of Christ as
second Adam is supported by this; it may indeed be
called an original find. Adam and Christ encompass
the two states of humanity: the fallen and the risen.
They not only symbolize it, but bring it about
through assimilation of humanity with their persons
(1 Cor. 15:21 ff. and 44-49; Rom. 5:12-21). Briefly,
Paul's idea is this: Through the first Adam, our
progenitor according to nature, we participate in
spiritual and bodily death. The task of the second
Adam, our progenitor according to the supernatural,
is therefore to release us from this spiritual and
bodily death.

The Redeemer indeed conquered sin through his
death on the cross, and bodily death through his
resurrection. The complete salvation act does not
consist in the death on the cross alone, but in the
death **and** resurrection. "Who was put to death for
our trespasses and raised for our justification" (Rom.
4:25). Are we not then redeemed through Jesus'
death on the cross? Without the slightest doubt!
But this redemption had to be applied to men individually. And this application, or with Paul this
"justification," was the act of the glorified Christ
who sent his Spirit to us. To be able to send him,
Christ himself first had to enter into his glory. For
Paul, the death and resurrection of Christ are the
answers to the double effect of justification: taking
away sin, and pouring in the new life.

The mystical body

The result of the redemption is what we commonly call the "mystical body." The term is taken from Paul, who presents the Church in the figure of a human body and further develops this concept in his letters from captivity: "Christ is the head of the body which is the Church." These three figures — Church as body, as body of Christ, and Christ as head — demand some explanation.

a. Why does Paul compare the Christendom of the Church with a body? Paul answers this in his extensive outline in 1 Cor. 12:12-30. Because we need to return to this text repeatedly, we here quote it in full: "(12) For just as the body is one and has many members, and all the members of the body, though many, are one body, so it is with Christ. (13) For by one Spirit we were all baptized into one body — Jews or Greeks, slaves or free — and all were made to drink of one Spirit. (14) For the body does not consist of one member but of many. (15) If the foot should say, Because I am not a hand, I do not belong to the body, that would not make it any less a part of the body. (16) And if the ear should say, Because I am not an eye, I do not belong to the body, that would not make it any less a part of the body. (17) If the whole body were an eye, where would be the hearing? If the whole body were an ear, where would be the sense of smell? (18) But as it is, God arranged the organs in the body, each one of them, as he chose. (19) If all were a single organ, where would the body be? (20) As it is, there are many parts, yet one body. (21) The eye cannot say to the hand, I have no need of you, nor again the head to the feet, I have no need of you. (22) On the contrary, the parts of the body which seem to be weaker are indispensable, (23) and those parts of the body which we think less honorable we invest with the greater honor, and our unpresentable parts are treated with greater modesty, (24) which our more presentable parts do not require. But God has so adjusted the body, giving the greater honor to the inferior part, (25) that there may be no discord in the body, but that the members may have the same care for one another. (26) If one member suffers, all suffer together: if one member is honored, all rejoice together. (27) Now you are the body of Christ and individually members of it. (28) And God has appointed in the church first apostles, second prophets, third teachers, then workers of miracles, then healers, helpers, administrators, speakers in various kinds of tongues. (29) Are all apostles? Are all prophets? Are all teachers? Do all work miracles? (30) Do all possess gifts of healing? Do all speak with tongues? Do all interpret?"

The outstanding feature in a human body — so the apostle argues — is the unity in multiplicity; in the multiplicity and diversity of organs a great unity and solidarity reveals itself. The same qualities one shall, indeed must, find in a well-ordered community. This Paul discovered precisely in the Christian community.

He saw in the Church a variegated mixture of

Jews and gentiles (vv. 13; cf. Eph. 2:11; 3:6), of
classes: slaves and free men (1, 13), but above all a
great variety of graces (vv. 27-30; cf. Rom. 12:6-8;
Eph. 4:11) from which the whole Church profits.

But for Paul diversity of members in the Church
does not exclude unity. He points out various factors
of unity in the immediate context of his statements
of the Church as body of Christ. We point out
some of them. In spite of their variety, graces have
the same origin (vv. 4-7; cf. Eph. 4:7, 11). Jew, Greek,
slave or free, all "are baptized by one Spirit into one
body" (v. 13). Jews and gentiles are "both reconciled
to God in one body through the Cross" (Eph. 2:16);
both have access to the Father in one Spirit (Eph.
2:18), are fellow heirs, members of the same body,
and partakers of the promise in Christ Jesus (Eph.
3:6). Furthermore they all partake of the one bread
of the Eucharist (1 Cor. 10:17) and their unity is
founded on "one body, one Spirit, one hope, one
Lord, one faith, one baptism, one God and Father
. . ." (Eph. 4:3-6). The composition of diversity and
unity in the same entity thus gave rise to the "body"
image.

b. Precisely why does Paul call the Church "the
body of Christ?" Three factors seem to have played
a part in this. In the first place this body is the
result of the redemptive work of Christ (Eph. 2:15
ff.) and so it has become his ·property, **his** body.
Further, it is animated by the Holy Spirit — more
exactly by the Spirit of Christ, the Spirit he infused
into it. Finally, there are two sacraments which

contribute in a special way to the unification of the
faithful: baptism and the Eucharist. When baptism
and Eucharist make the faithful mutually one, this
follows from their communion in Christ. For all
"have put on Christ" (Gal. 3:27) in baptism, and all,
through the Eucharistic food become, "partakers of
the body and blood of Christ."

There is no need to return to the redemption; the
Spirit and baptism will be dealt with separately later
on. "Communion" or joint presence at the Lord's
table is too important to the "body of Christ" to allow
us to pass it by in silence. "Because there is one
bread, we who are many are one body, for we all
partake of the one bread" (1 Cor. 10:17). We west-
erners cannot appreciate this. For easterners, especially for the Semites, the common table leads to
fraternization. Two people who share the same
bread draw, in a certain sense, their blood from the
same source; this inaugurates a friendship between
them, a family bond. If this symbol of fraternization
should, even for them, have lost much influence
through its conventional character, it nevertheless
becomes full reality when it concerns the Eucharistic
bread. Nothing less than Jesus' own body feeds all
guests unto eternal life and his blood flows through
their veins. What fraternity, what unity!

This is still more intensified by the sacrificial act.
When an Israelite brought his peace sacrifice, God
himself in a sense invited the faithful and served
them with his sacrificial food. So a unity "with the
altar" (1 Cor. 10:18) came about — a symbol of God

himself. As they felt themselves to be the children of God, so mutual love grew around the table of the common Father. The same applied to the pagan sacrificial meal; but this one led to "community with the devil." This religious table-community — for Israelites a source of mutual solidarity, for pagans a profanation through idolatry — becomes for Christians only, in the fullest sense, a "communion"; eating, now not the flesh of animals, but the very flesh and blood of the divine Sacrificial Lamb, makes the same blood, the same divine life flow through their veins as a firm bond of brotherhood; a solid unity is forged.

In view of this intimate union between faithful and Christ one can imagine how theologically charged are the appellations "body in Christ" and "body of Christ." They seem an answer to the often used Pauline formulas, "be in Christ" and "Christ in us." "Be in Christ" (164 times in Paul) usually has a mystical meaning. It always refers to the glorified Christ whose whole being — including his body — is so permeated with the divine power of the Spirit that he is spiritualized. "In Christ" therefore means that the faithful are taken into a new sphere of life through his baptism, have come into the sphere of influence and under the power of the personal Christ in his glorified existence. For this reason the first appellation "body in Christ" (Rom. 12:5) means that the massive body of the faithful subsists in the spiritual Christ, who is the source of its divine life and the origin of its moral action.

The second appellation "body of Christ" becomes
clear in the light of the formula "Christ in us." One
must not think of the Christ-living-in-us solely as an
impersonal power; it is Christ himself, in his glorified state. So "body of Christ" seems to say that the
spiritualized Christ is personally present and works
in the Church. The body which is the Church can
be called "of Christ," because he is its working
origin and he makes himself visible through her.

It is still not clear whether this "body of Christ"
is just a metaphor, as are "temple of God" and "a
pure virgin," or if it means more than these. We
believe that Paul sees more in it, and that he puts
it on the same level with Christ's human body, although — one must never overlook this — in a
mystical manner. The body of Christ, which the
faithful form, is in 1 Corinthians his mortal body
(12:13), or his Eucharistic body (10:17) or his carnal
body (6:15), though it is the source of spiritual life
(6:17). In the captivity letters the Church is identified with the heavenly and glorified body of Christ.
There is therefore a mystical equalization which is
more than just communion of life, yet less than
perfect identity. In view of the mystical in Paul's
theology (which makes for union), in view also of
the fact that the faithful die and rise in a mystical
manner with Christ — with the human body of the
personal Christ — and that they receive the "spiritual"
bread in the Eucharist, which is Christ's own body,
all requirements are, in our opinion, present to conclude to a **mystical** equalization of the Church as

"body of Christ" with the personal body of the
Redeemer. Confirmation of this may be found in
the fact that the Greeks never understood "body" as
a collective ("corporate body" is a modern notion),
but as an organism. If this is also Paul's viewpoint,
then we understand even better his preference for
this figure above all others; besides being a figure
it is also a reality, albeit a supernatural reality.

c. Why, finally, is Christ called "the head" of the
mystical body? What directly attracts our attention
in the letters to the Colossians and the Ephesians
is the relation Christ-Church — often expressed by
two terms: "head" and "fullness." As illustration,
we here use three texts from each of these letters.
"He is the **head** of the body, the Church; he is the
beginning, the first-born from the dead, that in
everything he might be pre-eminent. For in him all
the **fullness** of God was pleased to dwell" (Col. 1:18
ff.). "For in him the whole **fullness** of deity dwells
bodily, and you have come in fullness of life in him,
who is the head of all rule and authority" (Col.
2:9 ff.). "Let no one disqualify you, insisting on self-
abasement and worship of angels, taking his stand
on visions, . . . and not holding fast to the **head,** from
whom the whole body, nourished and knit together
through its joints and ligaments, grows with a growth
that is from God" (Col. 2:18 ff.). ". . . and he has put
all things under his feet and has made him the **head**
over all things for the Church, which is his body,
the **fullness** of him who fills all in all" (Eph. 1:22 ff.).
". . . and to know the love of Christ which surpasses
knowledge, that you may be filled with all the

fullness of God" (Eph. 3:19). ". . . until we all attain
to the unity of the faith and of the knowledge of
the Son of God, to mature manhood, to the measure
of the stature of the **fullness** of Christ . . . speaking
the truth in love, we are to grow up in every way
into him who is the **head,** into Christ" (Eph. 4:13-16).

Careful reading of these texts brings certain facts
to light. In Colossae a kind of worship of angels is
in vogue (Col. 2:18 ff.). These angels would —
probably together with Christ — exercise mediation
and are qualified with "fullness," the sum total of
divine powers. Certain that this doctrine detracts
from the role of Christ, Paul emphasizes that Christ
is exclusively the bearer of the highest authority as
well as of the office of mediator. To account for
this double function in Christ he adopts from his adversaries the word "fullness" and applies it to Christ.
As Christ possesses the fullness of the Godhead (Col.
2:19), he is above the universe and merits in truth
the name "head" or Lord of the angels (Col. 2:10)
as well as of the Church (Col. 1:18; 2:19). Because
Christ possesses this fullness, the Church, which is
one with him, becomes its reservoir: in other words,
his divine treasures of grace are constantly contained
in her. In this respect "head" means the principle of
solidarity and growth of life. Paul wishes that the
Ephesians "may be filled with all the fullness of
God" and all attain to mature manhood, "to the
measure of the stature of the fullness of Christ" (Eph.
3:19; 4:13); he instructs them that God has given
Christ as head of the Church, which is his body,

"the fullness of him who fills all in all" (Eph. 1:23).
It does not matter if this role reaches further than
what physiology awards the head in relation to the
body; for Paul all growth of the body, all the Church
possesses in life, power, beauty, harmony and perfection springs from the life-giving and constant influence of Christ; in this function he calls Christ
"head."

Origin and development

In speaking about the **origin and the development**
of the metaphor of the mystical body, I would like
to begin with the latter.

A certain development may be deduced in the
phraseology of Paul. The great letters use the term
"body" only for the local community (1 Cor. 6:15;
10:17; 12:3, 27; Rom. 12:5); they call this by way of
exception "body of (in) Christ" (1 Cor. 12:27; Rom.
2:5). But they are silent about Christ's role in that
body, so that he is more or less hidden ("immanence").
The captivity letters however use "body" only for
the universal Church (Col. 1:18; 2 ff.; Eph. 1:23 ff.);
they emphatically identify it as the "body of Christ"
and adjudicate the role of "head" to Christ himself
("transcendence").

The body metaphor was nothing new; it was com-
monplace with the Greeks. They often compare the
state with a body and its members; Plato did it,
Aristotle did it; it is preserved for us in its classical
form in the well known fable of Menenius Agrippa.
The Greeks also wanted to make Peloppponnesus

"a body"; vine and branches form one body; an
address or a melody can consist of one body or
separate parts; etc.

Since the metaphor does not appear in the Old
or in the New Testament, Paul certainly borrowed
it from the Greek world. The whole depiction in
1 Cor. 12 — the text in which the body-metaphor
first appears — namely the body as an organic unity
(vv. 14-20), the members of which depend on one
another (21-25), and especially share in one another's
suffering and joy (25), is common in the Stoics. Add
to this that in Paul, as well as with the Stoics, the
metaphor has a moralizing function and was considered to be a stimulus to unity (also in Rom. 12:3-8
and elsewhere), then this would cover the whole
field.

But hellenistic influence does not explain everything. For the Greeks, "body" meant no more than
the state, or humanity or the cosmos, in which one
traces profane activity. In Paul however it is the
Christian community in which the Spirit works and
distributes charismata, and is closely connected with
Christ. Paul therefore sublimates the hellenistic
theme by building it into his Christology. At first
the wording is still uncertain and variable: "so with
Christ," "body of Christ," "body in Christ" (1 Cor.
12:12, 27; Rom. 12:5). Later in the captivity letters
it has become a current expression: "the body of
Christ." The factor which brought Paul to introduce
the Church as the body of Christ is without a doubt
his doctrine of the mystical union of the faithful with

Christ — this certainly came first; added to this is his doctrine about the Eucharist.

That the function of Christ concerning his body was later expressed through the metaphor "head," owes its origin to apologetics. As indicated, in Colossians and Ephesians one must distinguish between **what** Paul taught and **how** he did it. The objective doctrine is that Christ is the principle of leadership, solidarity, and life. The objective wording is that this threefold function is symbolized by the term "head"; the foundation upon which he leans (Christ's divinity and fullness of grace) is expressed by "fullness." "Head" and "fullness," in this pregnant meaning, appear exclusively in the letters to the Colossians and Ephesians.

Holy Spirit

If the Son is the head, the Spirit is the **soul** of the mystical body. "For by one Spirit we were all baptized into one body, Jews and Greeks, slaves or free, and all were made to drink of one Spirit" (1 Cor. 12:13), "one body and one spirit" (Eph. 4:3 ff.). In the Spirit and through his action the "temple" originates; at one time this images the Church in her universality (Eph. 2:22), at another time a local community (1 Cor. 10:17), elsewhere again the faithful (1 Cor. 6:19: "Do you not know that your body is a temple of the Holy Spirit").

As soul of the mystical body the Spirit is the constitutional and inspiring principle: constitutional through his unifying power, inspiring by caring for the unfolding of divine life in the Church.

Most of Paul's letters begin with a thanksgiving to God for the spiritual advancement of the readers. He always points to the growth of their faith, their hope, and their love. In his opinion, spiritual life is the same as the life of the three divine virtues. To trace how, in his estimation, the Spirit works at unfolding the divine life in the Church, we can do no better than to follow his actions in this threefold field.

a. As the term **faith** indicates now the beginning, now an enduring state so, in regard to the Holy Spirit, we can speak of an infusion or of an inhabitation.

Infusion of the Spirit, because it has taken place in the past, is always expressed in the past tense: the Spirit which has been given to us (Rom. 5:5), has been sent (Gal. 4:6), was received by the faithful (1 Thess. 1:6; Gal. 3:2), were washed, sanctified, justified (1 Cor. 6:11) and were sealed (Eph. 1:13).

In 1 Cor. 2 we read how this infusion takes place. First, it is exclusively the Spirit of God who fathoms the divine mysteries; he alone therefore can reveal to the apostles what they are to preach. "God has revealed to us (apostles) through the Spirit. For the Spirit searches everything, even the depths of God. . . . no one comprehends the thoughts of God except the Spirit of God" (1 Cor. 2:10-12; cf. Eph. 3:5). The Spirit not only imparts the message to the apostles; he also provides for their delivery. "We impart this in words not taught by human wisdom but taught by the Spirit, interpreting spiritual truths to those who possess the Spirit" (1 Cor. 2:13; cf. 1 Cor. 2:3-5; 2 Cor. 3:5 ff.; 1 Thess. 1:5; cf. Mt. 10:20). But the same Spirit must attune the audience to the preaching. "The unspiritual man does not receive the gifts of the Spirit of God, for they are folly to him, and he is not able to understand them because they are spiritually discerned" (1 Cor. 2:14). "And you became imitators of us and of the Lord, for you received the word in much affliction, with joy inspired by the Holy Spirit" (1 Thess. 1:6; cf. Gal. 3:2).

There are therefore three aspects in the communication of the Holy Spirit: revelation, preaching, and infusion with supernatural symptoms of joy and peace. All three can be reduced to the activity of the Spirit. Without the Spirit therefore no one can come to the faith (1 Cor. 12:3).

This is not all. The act of faith is followed by the virtue of faith. Here the Spirit works through enlightenment (Col. 1:9 ff.; Eph. 1:17 ff.). There is one condition: our faith must not be sterile, but active through love (Eph. 1:15: "because" . . . ; 3:17 ff.). The reason for this is that the Spirit works in two domains at the same time: upon the mind and upon the will. If we restrain his action on ethical grounds, we simultaneously impede him in the field of enlightenment (cf. 1 Cor. 2:3; especially 2:6 "the mature"; and 3:1, "the spiritual men").

b. The Spirit also activates our virture of **hope;** as the divine Gift he opens eschatological perspectives.

"The Spirit himself bearing witness with our spirit, that we are children of God, and if children then heirs . . ." (Rom. 8:16 ff.). We possess evidence of this inheritance. The presence of the Spirit is "the first fruit" for us (Rom. 8:23), and at the same time a guarantee and "partial dividend" (2 Cor. 1:21; 5:5) of our heavenly inheritance (Eph. 1:4) and of our bodily resurrection (Rom. 8:11; Eph. 4:30). On God's part, presence of the Spirit means a claim upon us: he is the "seal" of God's property (Eph. 1:13; 4:30). For this reason the Spirit is the principle of hope for the whole Church (Rom. 15:30; Eph. 4:4).

Between infusion of the Spirit and the payment of our inheritance lies the time, when the Spirit lives in us as our guest (Rom. 8:9 ff.; 1 Cor. 3:16) where he exercises his activity. His indwelling effects our being children of God (Rom. 8:15 ff.): "all who are led by the Spirit of God are Sons of God" (Rom. 8:14). Next to the eschatological moment stands the actual moment; next to a guarantee of the future, the Spirit living in us is simultaneously the power-plant of our spiritual life (Eph. 3:16) which unites us with Christ (1 Cor. 6:17; Rom. 8:9) and renews us indeed (Tit. 3:5). He effects this renewal by praying in and for us (Rom. 8:26 ff.) or by making our lives agreeable through justification, peace and joy (Rom. 14:17); under his guidance we are also able to bridle the desires of the flesh (Rom. 8:9-10 and 13-14), to serve God (Phil. 3:3) and to model ourselves on Christ (2 Cor. 3:18). We must therefore take care not to grieve the Holy Spirit of God through sin (Eph. 4:30).

c. Finally, the Spirit is equally the principle of **love.** "God's love has been poured into our hearts through the Holy Spirit which has been given us" (Rom. 5:5). "I appeal to you, brethren, by our Lord Jesus Christ and by the love of the Spirit" (Rom. 15:30).

The "building up of the body in the Spirit" is practically considered as "the building up of the body in love" (cf. Eph. 2:22 with 4:16). The Spirit demands that Christians help each other. His own contribution consists in the charismata — favors he bestows on privileged persons for the welfare of all (1 Cor. 12:4, 7, 11, etc.); because of their origin they are also called spiritual gifts (1 Cor. 12:1; 14:1). From the fourfold summary which Paul gives (1 Cor. 12:8-10 and 28-30; Rom. 12:6-9; Eph. 4:11) — repeatedly mentioned in one breath with the "body of Christ" — their importance for the Church is evident. "Joints and ligaments" which connect Head and members also seem to allude to charismatic gifts (Col. 2:19; Eph. 4:16). Paul himself enjoyed these spiritual gifts in high degree (1 Cor. 14:18). Under no circumstances does he want them suppressed (1 Thess. 5:19 ff.).

The distinction in the Church between the institutional-hierarchical and the free charismata is very real. God's Spirit dwells where he wills. For the underprivileged and poor, for women and children, for laymen without office — in short, for every member of the Church — there can be a mission in the Kingdom of God. Free charismatics must live in peace with Church officials. These latter for their part must judge, with the charism of discernment, the action of the Spirit in these free charismatics and accommodate it to the benefit of the Church. Only with this non-institutional essential can the Church be, in accordance with Christ's will, what she must be — and through his Spirit will be.

In the history of the Church, official and free charismatic gifts were often found in one and the same person. But God does not will that the officials of his Church are always the most favored with charismata, or that the most favored charismatics by this same token are always vested with the highest offices. Hence the Church can be rightly judged only when she is seen as the union of office and charism willed by God. From neither office or charism may we desire or expect that which we would wish to find in both.

Summarizing, we may say: the Holy Spirit is light, he is vitality and guarantee, he is the bond of love of Christ and neighbor. Here we very closely approach the theology of John.

Christian life

God himself builds his Church. He begins with loving choice and efficacious calling (2 Thess. 2:13 ff.; Rom. 8:28 ff.; Eph. 1:4); hence Christians are still called "chosen ones" (Col. 3:12) and the "called" (1 Cor. 1:2; Rom. 1:6). God further constructs through his word the divine message which demands our faith; from this comes the name the "faithful."

God takes these faithful into the Church through baptism.

". . . You were buried with him in **baptism,** in which you were also raised with him through **faith** in the working of God, who raised him from the dead" (Col. 2:12 ff.). "For in Christ Jesus you are all sons of God through **faith,** for as many of you as were **baptized** into Christ have put on Christ" (Gal. 3:26).

That faith and baptism are the two requisites for admittance into the Church is nothing new. Jesus himself had already said: "He who believes and is baptized, will be saved" (Mk. 16:16); and to Nicodemus he said: "Unless one is born of water and the Spirit, he cannot enter the Kingdom of God . . . that whoever believes in him may have eternal life" (Jn. 3:5, 15). The first Church identified with this: "Those who received (believed) the word were baptized . . ." (Acts 2:41); the same thing happened in Samaria and to the Ethiopan (Acts 8:12, 36-38).

Faith and baptism as the two factors of Christianization are therefore traditional. Paul however is original in his antithesis between the old and the new salvation order to which he constantly refers (Col. 2:11-14; Gal. 3:23-29; Rom. 6:3-16).

Here is his usual schema:

	mediator	sub. element	obj. element
(O.T.)	The Law	works (of the Law)	circumcision
(N.T.)	Christ	faith	baptism

Another original trait in Paul is that he clarifies the connection between faith and baptism. From the texts quoted above it is evident that faith is internal, an active readiness, a personal attitude. Baptism however is external, a rite one undergoes. Of these two, baptism, not faith, is the real incorporation. In his schema baptism corresponds with circumcision; as this was incorporation into the Old Israel, baptism is into the New Israel, the Church. Thus the apostle can say: "For as many of you as were baptized into Christ have put on Christ" (Gal. 3:27).

Faith disposes to incorporation. By faith the apostle understands above all a response to the Christian message: "Whether then it was I or they, so we preach and so you believed" (1 Cor. 15:11). The beginning act of faith has privileges; this is why Paul makes it distinct from the virtue of faith. The beginning act points to justification (Rom. 3:21-27; Gal. 2:16-21), as the case of Abraham, prefigure of the faithful, indicates (Gal. 3:6); it also points to baptism (Eph. 1:13).

By baptism we enter into personal union with Christ; we become his possession and enter into his service. In the Pauline perspective of the mystical body this means the same as incorporation. We read in 1 Cor. 1:10-17, how baptism joins one much more closely with Christ than pupil with master. The Corinthians indulged in personality-cult; everyone adhered to one or other favorite teacher. Stupid! says Paul, for the One to whom all belong is Christ. Why? He alone was crucified for them and they are baptized in his name alone (v. 13). Don't swear therefore by the servants, when actually you belong to the Master. Later in the same letter we read how the Israelites became one people through their leader (10:2: "and all were baptized into Moses in the cloud and in the sea") as a prefiguration of the unification of the faithful in Christ. Emphasizing this mystical trait, Gal. 3:27 points to a transformation of man: "For as many of you as were baptized into Christ, have put on Christ." Here unity of nature is an effect of mystical identification with Christ. In Tit. 3:5-8, finally, we find how baptism is at the same time a cleansing-bath (as in Eph. 5:26) and regeneration. Regeneration is presented as the work of the three divine persons: "God saved us . . . by the washing of regeneration and renewal in the Holy Spirit, which he poured out upon us richly through Jesus Christ, our Savior." Could one find a more eloquent commentary on the mandate given to the apostle to baptize in the name of the Father and the Son and the Holy Spirit?

Doubtless, there is incorporation. But how does the apostle picture this mysterious unification with Christ? He offers his most beautiful exposition in Rom. 5:3-11: "baptized in Christ" (vv. 3 and 5). Submission of the disciple in the baptismal water, he teaches us, represents the death and burial of Christ; his rising from the water imitates the resurrection of the Redeemer. This is not mere symbolism. The baptized undergoes the death and resurrection of

Christ so strongly that he really participates in the
death of the cross and resurrection. Thus a mystical
unification takes place; although internal and hidden,
it is nevertheless real. Through the power of Christ's
merits the baptized really "dies" to sin and to his
sinful desires. There is this difference: while his
guilt of sin vanishes at once, his concupiscence
(called by Paul "the old man," "the body of sin")
is overcome only gradually, while the inclination to
evil still lives on in the reborn man. But this concupiscence has received a mortal blow, for it is debilitated
by grace. At the same time however, the baptized
"rises" to a new, a divine life, by which the victorious
Christ transforms his soul in anticipation that one
day — the last day — his body too will share in this
divinity (cf. Rom. 8:11; Phil. 3:20 ff.).

The **new life** of the baptized must, like all life,
be brought to fruition. The objective-sacramental
effect must now be lived on a subjective-ethical
level. This means: whatever sacramental grace has
been embodied in us from without, must now be
given formulation from within by our cooperation.

This can be further elucidated. As was mentioned,
there are in our salvation economy two progenitors:
Adam and Christ. From Adam we received "sin,"
from Christ "life." From Adam we received "the
old man" of concupiscence, from Christ "the new
man" of grace. As Adam passed on natural life, the
old man lived "according to the flesh"; as Christ
passed on supernatural life, the new man lives "according to the spirit." This new baptismal life aspires

to baptismal living. What was received once, must be permanently cultivated. This is a repeatedly recurring motif in Paul's exhortations.

Col. 3:1-12 is an example. Though risen, though living with Christ, the readers are nevertheless urged to "seek" supernatural things (v. 1); though dead (v. 3) they must still die (v. 5); though they have put on the new man (v. 10) they must put on more of him (v. 12). It is obvious that the old and new man here indicate states of sinfulness and sanctity. Paul compares them with two coats, one to be taken off, the other to be put on. The new one differs radically from the old; growth takes place gradually, as is evident from his use of the present participle "being renewed"(10). The model here is God (v. 10; Eph. 4:24; 5:1); or, more clearly Christ (Phil. 2:3-5; Eph. 5:2; 4:12 ff.) or his faithful image, Paul (Phil. 4:9 etc.). This new man is distinct from the old in a practical sense because of his new insights (v. 16) and his moral conduct (v. 12 in comp. v. 8; cf. Eph. 4:20-24).

6

BIBLICAL - THEOLOGICAL SYNTHESIS

Our inquiry is not complete; in order not to become too diffuse we have not discussed the Catholic letters and Revelation; actually, these are of minor importance for our purpose. We will now try to arrange the compiled data.

The essence of the Church

The name "Church" or "community of God" is not found in most New Testament writings. But the idea is present everywhere, under constantly changing figures. The synoptics speak of a flock, a city or a mountain, a fishing net, a vineyard, a tree whereon all birds make their nests; the synoptics and Paul speak of a people, a kingdom, a bride; Peter and Paul refer to a temple; Paul mentions a body with members, John a vine with branches. These concepts — excepting "body" — originally are Old Testament, and are consciously carried over from the old Israel to the new. This name-transfer points to continuity with the old Israel and it implies that the heir is a new community.

There is **continuity**, because God is faithful to the

promises he once made (Rom. 11). The prophecies
are fulfilled in Jesus Christ, one of the chosen race,
and in the communication of the Holy Spirit; this
means that God has poured out the promised salvific goods over humanity in and through the mediator, Christ. Although the number of Jews who
accepted him was small (announced by the prophets
as the cleansed "remnant") they are needed; only by
union with them can the gentiles become a real
"Israel." The nucleus of the new Israel is the apostles
who through their number symbolize the twelve
patriarchs of the old Israel. Curiously enough they
confine their efforts almost exclusively to Judaism
in and outside Palestine. Even the "apostle of the
gentiles" submits his gospel to Jerusalem for approval,
sends the proceeds of his collections to the poor
of that city. In his mission work the Jews come
first (Acts 13:46; 14:1; 16:13 ff.; Rom. 1:16). Non-Jews
are reminded that they are graftings on the old vine
and that the old torn-off branches can be restored:
the Jews shall again be received in the end time
(Rom. 1:17-29; cf. Eph. 2:14-18).

So a **third genus,** a new generation comes into
being, that is no longer Jewish or gentile but just
Christian. In the beginning of the Acts the new
community clearly differs from the old because she
has her own faith (Christian), her own means of
grace (sacraments) and her own government (apostles, later also deacons and elders). Through these
three factors the Christian community is welded
into a solid unity. It is practically impossible to say

where this unity comes to the fore most strongly: in the four gospels, in the Acts and in Paul, the texts are overwhelming. Love is the main commandment of Christ, the jewel of the primeval community, the key word of Paul. The Church is holy through evangelical doctrine which preaches perfection: holy also through her faith and sacraments (especially baptism and Eucharist) which connect her members with the Redeemer: holy, finally, through the Holy Spirit working in her, and because of her eschatological attitude. Her catholic character, her being open to the whole of humanity, was the explicit will of her Founder, the main theme of the Acts and the life aim of the apostle of the gentiles. Her apostolicity in maintained through her fidelity to the original teaching and the unbroken succession of government in the Church.

At first this government existed in the college of the apostles. The gospels narrate their selection, their formation, their privileged position, their mission. The Acts portrays them as witnesses of Christ, workers of miracles and rulers of the young Church; the prominence given to Peter, James and John put their colleagues in the shadows. In Ephesians Paul calls them the foundation on which the Church is built, and in Galatians he refers to them as pillars of the Church. A unique place is allotted to Peter. Three gospels mention his elevation to the primacy, four apostle-lists place him in the top position. In the Acts we see him as head of the twelve take the initiative over and over again; ten of his orations

are mentioned; at the council of Jerusalem he takes
the lead. Paul too, as is evident, acknowledged him
as leader (Gal. 1:18; 2:8). To hold that the hierarchy
died out with the death of the last apostle is without
solid foundation. The Petrine-text with the promise
that the Church shall never succumb, the mission
text with the promise that Christ will assist his
emissaries to the end of the world, the Israelitic
tradition that the people of God is not imaginable
without leadership — in fine, the logic which indicates that the government instituted by Christ was
on behalf of the Church and therefore an essential
element — all these point to the untenability of the
position that the apostolicity of the Church would
be a question only of doctrinal content, and not
at the same time concern succession.

That the apostolic Church possessed a hierarchy
is therefore undeniable. That the apostles through
laying on of hands provided themselves with official
cooperators, can also be ascertained from several
texts (Acts 14:23; 1 Tim. 5:17-22; Tit. 1:5). This
ceremony indicates that the office required a special
charism of the Holy Spirit: it is therefore not just
a function of government. In the letters of James
one sees the presbyters praying for the sick and
anointing them with holy oil (James 5:14). Nevertheless they were also local leaders (1 Tim. 5:17), as
the appellation "chairmen" (**proistamenos:** 1 Thess.
5:12 ff.; Rom. 12:8) as well as "leaders" (**hiegoumenos:**
Heb. 13:7, 17, 24) would seem to indicate. One must
admit that the appellation for the lower hierarchy

in apostolic times was still casual; the terms **episkopos** and **presbyteri** seem interchangeable (Acts 20:17, 28; Tit. 1:5, 7; 1 Tim. 5:17). Some, like Spieg and Gaechter, claim to see here a clear reference to the episcopate.

A special characteristic which the Constiution on the Church (Nos. 22-23) states concerning the episcopate is its **collegiality.** On this we offer a short elucidation.

The pope is the successor of Peter; but we cannot say that a bishop is the successor of any particular apostle. The college of bishops as a whole succeeds the college of the apostles. The consecration of a bishop is the sacrament whereby he is taken into the college of bishops which as a unit is the continuation of the college of apostles. For this reason the episcopal consecration from ancient times always takes place through the laying on of hands by three bishops; this signifies that the consecrated one is taken **by** the college **into** the college. To make this even more clear the new rulings of Vatican II insist that, from now on all other bishops present will lay on their hands. A bishop is therefore, above all, a member of this college, which together with the pope governs, teaches and sanctifies the whole Church. The Church is therefore not governed by one man, the pope, but by the college of bishops to which the pope belongs as the head. This is by institution of Christ himself. The pope receives his authority directly from Christ himself; bishops also, through the consecration sacrament, receive their authority from Christ and not from the pope. The pope cannot pretend that the college of bishops does not exist. To be pope means to be within the college of bishops as head of this college and therefore as chief shepherd of the Church. Without college there is no pope; without the pope there is no college either. The pope is the principle of unity, the connecting center to which the whole college is directed and in which it finds its function. The Pope possesses highest authority over the whole Church as head of the college of bishops, therefore not without this college; the Acts mention "Peter and the eleven." Bishops possess the same supreme authority — not each one separately, but only as college and then only when in union with the head. Pope and world-episcopate are mutually conjoined, are dependent on one another. The pope does not stand in opposition to the college of bishops but within it.

The Church is therefore not a monarchy, a government by one; neither is it a democracy: it is not comparable with any worldly form of government; it has its own unique form. One might therefore raise objections to the word "college": juridically speaking, a college is a group of equals; this is not the case here. That the bishops together form a college, corporately and with the pope, as the Council states in the third chapter, was never really a problem. The question is: does the pope as supreme pastor belong to the college? This question is left open by the Council; for the present one may think of this as one pleases.

A second question is the priesthood of the laity, concerning which much has been said. Some contemporaries go so far as to confuse the boundaries of the ministerial priesthood: The believing layman, they say, can confer several sacraments: he can baptize validly, with his partner he confects the sacrament of marriage; is it possible that, in an emergency, he would be able to give absolution from sin? etc.? Thus the ecclesiastical office becomes problematical. This is why the Constitution on the Church devotes no less than three chapters to it (Nos. 10-12; see also Nos. 34-38).

In the Gospels investigated, and in the Acts and Letters of Paul, the title "royal priesthood" of the laity does not occur. Jesus does not call the people priestly, nor himself a priest. Yet he is a priest and it would seem that he regarded the people of the New Covenant as a priestly people. Jesus makes himself known as priest through the sacrifice of his life and the office of the Word. It is noteworthy that he also invites his followers to share in both these priestly functions: every disciple must take up his cross (Mt. 16:24 par.) and drink his chalice (Lk. 9:60; 10:1-16), bear testimony of him to the death (Mt. 10:16-42). When Jesus imparted to all men his titles of Son and King, he made them all priests.

The classic text is 1 Pet. 2:5, 9, where the people of God are called "a holy priesthood" a "royal priesthood" (cf. Rev. 1:6; 5:10; 20:6; and Ex. 19:3-6). But this "royal priesthood" always had a figurative mean-

ing in the age-old prehistory. The worship to which
the people of Exodus were called could not have
been a sacrifice in the strict sense; an official priesthood was appointed for that. The appellation was
therefore spiritualized and remained so in Is. 61:6,
in the Judaism of Alexandria and in the apocalyptic
literature. Israel was to bring the word of the true
God to the pagan peoples and secure his worship
among them; this task was later taken up by Christianity. When the New Testament made use of the
formula of Exodus it was already laden with the
weight of history.

1 Peter faithfully follows this tradition; the book of
Revelation sees the people as liturgical in a strict
sense — but this occurs only in heaven. 1 Peter
decidedly follows in the context of a spiritualized
priesthood. The whole narrative (1 Pet. 2:1-10) is
a moralizing warning which points to this: the
Sonship is **spiritual** (v. 2); the living stones (4-8,
namely the faithful) are **spiritual** and the temple
which they form is explicitly called a **spiritual** temple
(5, namely the Church); the holy priesthood offers
spiritual sacrifices (5); these are internal sacrifices:
good works and suffering in imitation of Christ 2:20;
prayer 3:7; 4:7; love which cleanses from sin: 4:8.
Why not also the "royal priesthood" mentioned in
(9)? This royal priesthood must be spiritual too, in
contrast with the material priesthood of the old
ritual. The triad — temple, offering and priesthood
— is therefore a metaphor based on the Old Testament temple, offering and priest. The formula

"through Jesus Christ" (5) points to the fact that, thanks to him and in union with him, Christians offer of God a new cult.

When Christians compare their religion with Judaism or paganism, they are perfectly correct in introducing their own religion as one which has a spiritual nature. Their worship is really and exclusively in spirit and truth. We find this spiritualized cult of the Christian people in Paul (cf. Eph. 2:18 ff.; Phil. 3:3; Rom. 12:1). But above this the Christian people possess, in the passion of Christ, in the Eucharist and in the hierarchy, a new reason to see their religion as a priesthood and an offering. In this perspective it is not surprising therefore that the Constitution on the Church (Nos. 10-12) goes no further than to give the laity as such a spiritual priesthood.

Initiative of the Father

The Constitution on the Church begins with the Church and the Holy Trinity (Nos. 2-4); we would like to end this little work on the same note.

The salvation mystery of Paul makes it clear that all salvific initiative comes from God. To save in and through Christ the whole of humanity without distinction of race, status or culture, was from all eternity the ordinance of the immeasurable goodness of God. It is he who sent his Son, according to Paul and John. Not surprisingly, the Son therefore announced the "Kingdom of God," as the gospels call it; Paul, who prefers to speak of the Church, calls this the "Church of God" but never "Church of Christ."

God sent his Son; and according to the ancient formula of the Acts, it was God who worked in and through Christ. So Peter declares that God confirmed the mission of Jesus of Nazareth, performed miracles through him, decreed his condemnation, raised him, placed him at his right hand and gave him the promised Spirit; in short, God made him Lord and Christ (Acts 2:22-36; cf. 3:13 ff.) — Paul for his part confirms this salvific initiative of the Father. The salvation decree went out from him; in his Son, he reconciled the world to himself (2 Cor. 5:18 ff.). But he did more! The sanctification itself ultimately comes from him as he places his enormous power at the service of Christians (Eph. 1:19; 3:16, 20; 6:10). Paul may sow, Apollo water, but God gives growth to the Church (1 Cor. 3:6) and his omnipotence, which raised Christ and crowned him with glory (Eph. 1:20-22), has in and with him "raised us up and made us sit in the heavenly places" (Eph. 2:6). Nowhere does he characterize God's salvific initiative as typically as he does in the opening hymn of the letter to Epheisians and in the concise words of Rom. 8:28-30.

In the opening hymn of Ephesians and elsewhere, Paul always prays to the Father; and the primeval community prays with him. This is the Judaic influence; in their devotional life the Son did not relegate the Father into the background. The only thing new of the old-Christian prayer is its dependence on the mediation of Christ: "through Christ our Lord."

Mediation of the Son

"Through our Lord Jesus Christ," mediator between God and men — this best characterizes the role of Christ.

The synoptic gospels especially present Jesus as the mediator-prophet who announces the Kingdom of God, performs miracles to introduce it, promulgates the new law of God, forgives sins with divine authority, and works "for" the people (Mk. 10:45) with a humility and an obedience which brings him to a cross.

The primeval community sees in Jesus the Messiah, the King of the end time expected by the Jews but, more particularly, the heavenly king. The sermons in the Acts all follow the same theme: Jesus suffered and died; he arose and was glorified. In this ancient preaching the accent is placed on his glory, not on his suffering. We hear little of a redemption through death on a cross; salvation is rather a gift from the risen and glorified Christ (Acts 5:31).

Paul too uses the theme death-resurrection-glory as the formula of the one great salvation mystery. He goes a step further: he presents the redemptive value of Christ's passion to full advantage; in this

connection, it is not mere chance that the term
"Redeemer," twice mentioned in the gospels and
twice in Acts appears in Paul twelve times. However with him too the resurrection is not just an
appendix! Jesus returned to the Father not by his
death alone but by his death and his resurrection;
so he also leads us back to God not only by taking
away our sins but by taking away sins and infusion
of the new life. This latter is the life of the risen
Christ. Precisely in his risen state Christ simultaneously becomes our Lord **and** the source of life
from which the treasures of grace flow to us; both
functions meet in the new name "Head" which is
due to him because of his body the Church.

Sanctification through the Spirit

The Father takes the initiative, he is the origin
and executor of the salvific plan; the Son, as God
made man, is his instrument of redemption; but who
or what is the Holy Spirit?

At his departure Jesus promised his disciples a
Helper. On the first Pentecost, birthday of the
Church, he fulfilled this promise. In conjunction
with the third gospel, which more than the others
stresses the influence of the Spirit on Jesus' appear-
ance (4:1, 14, 18; 10:21), the Acts give the impression
that the young Church was strongly influenced by
the operation of the Spirit — so much so that this
book has often been called the gospel of the Holy
Spirit. The nature of his operation appears to be
principally charismatic; the leaders are enlightened
and strengthened, many of the faithful receive charis-

mata: speaking with tongues, prophecy and the gift of performing miracles — all this directed to the welfare and extension of the Church. Nothing is said of the sanctifying work of the Spirit, at least not explicitly. Incidentally, we are told that Ananias and Saphira "lie to the Holy Spirit, to tempt the Spirit" (5:3, 9) and that the persecutors of Stephen "resist the Holy Spirit" (7:51); also that the two descriptions of the growth of the primeval community (2:42-47 and 4:32-35) follow upon an infusion of the Spirit. But again, all this is as nothing in comparison with the great charismatic force of the Spirit.

This changes in Paul. He too certainly speaks of charismatic working, but for him this is integrated into the great salvation process which the Spirit performs in the Church. The apostles receive from the Spirit the content and form of their preaching: he calls the hearers to the act of faith, and is infused in them; once received, he is the principle of the deepening of faith and moral growth in the Christian. As seal of God's property and pledge of future inheritance, the Spirit is our warranty, our title of hope. As bond of love he keeps the children of God together in that great body of Christ, which he constructs through his charismata of mutual helpfulness and keeps intimately connected with the Head, Christ.

Finally, it is the apostle himself who in 1 Cor. 6:11 formulates the Trinity identification with the Church: "You were washed, you were sanctified,

you were justified (the work of God) in the name
of the Lord Jesus Christ (as mediator) and in the
Spirit of our God (as sanctifier). We know no better
way to end than to make his paean ours:

> O the depths of the riches and wisdom
>   and knowledge of God!
> How unsearchable are his judgments
>   and how inscrutable his ways!
>   (Romans 11:33)

BIBLIOGRAPHY

Dictionnaire biblique Vigouroux, Supplément 487-687: 'Eglise'

Theologisches Wörterbuch zum Neuen Testament, several articles

Vocabulaire Biblique (Neuchatel): Eglise, Espirit, Royaume

Bijbels Woordenboek 2 (Roermond): Kerk

F. Prat, Théologie de Saint Paul, Paris 1924

F. Jügensmeier, Het mystieke lichaam van Christus (Transl. from German) Bosch 1936

A. Wikenhauser, Die Kirche als der Mystieke Leib Christi nach dem Apostel Paulus (Münster i. W.) 1937

E. Mersch, Le corps mystique du Christ

L. Cerfaux, La théologie de l'Eglise suivant Saint Paul Paris 1942

E. Schillebeekx Tijdschrift voor Theologie 1965 pp. 297-298 Paris 1949

W. Goosens, L'Eglise corps du Christ d'après Saint Paul Paris 1949

H. Schlier, Die Zeit der Kirche (Freiburg i. B.) 1956

Ned. Kath. Stemmen 1958, p. 97 (J. Kahmann)

Ned. Kath. Stemmen 1953, p. 109

Het Schild 1960, p. 121 (J. Kahmann)

Collationes Brugenses et Gandavenses 1956, p. 463 (B. Willaert)

Introduction à la Bible, II Nouveau Testament (Paris 1959) Thèmes majeurs, p. 771

   Dogmatic Constitution in the Church (Vatican II, 1965)